How to cope with worry

Janet Haines
Mandy Matthewson

Acknowledgements:
Steven Haines
Robyn Cartledge
Coverart designed by Freepik
(www.freepik.com)

This workbook offers suggestions on how to cope with your tendency to worry. We do not guarantee that these suggested strategies will resolve all psychological symptoms. You may wish to seek alternative assistance from a mental health professional.

How to cope with worry
Janet Haines & Mandy Matthewson
Copyright © 2025
ISBN: 978-1-923573-19-2

About the authors

Dr Janet Haines has a PhD in Clinical Psychology and has worked as an academic and researcher for 17 years, and in private practice for 30 years helping people facing life problems.

Dr Mandy Matthewson is a Clinical Psychologist, educator and researcher with more than two decades of experience supporting people through life's toughest challenges.

For S. So many worries for one so young.
For G, who later in life realised she could just let go.

Table of contents

Table of contents 5
Introduction 7
What you need to know about worry 8
The features of worry 9
    Catastrophising 9
    Increased anxiety 9
    Inability to tolerate uncertainty 9
    Problems accepting risk 10
    Unsuccessful problem solving 10
    Trying to achieve perfection 10
    Unhelpful beliefs related to worry 11
    Failure to control worry 11
    Worrying about worrying 11
The things you worry about 13
Differences between good and bad worry 14
What is the difference between worrying and problem-solving? 16
The link between worry and Generalised Anxiety Disorder 18
What you need to know about anxiety 19
    What is my nervous system doing? 19
    Range of arousal 21
The problem of attention and concentration 24
    How these problems manifest 24
    Causes of the problem 25
    How can I fix this? 27
Is it safe to stop worrying? 28
How can I stop worrying? 29
How to combat anxiety 30
    More exercises to help 36
    Managing anxiety-related thoughts 38
How to combat worry 43

- Worry control strategies 43
  - Interrupting the cycle 46
- Dealing with sleep disturbance 48
  - What can I do about my sleep problems? 50
- A worry decision tree 52
- Worry, emotion and behaviour 54
- Managing uncertainty 57
  - Challenging your uncertainty 57
  - Accepting uncertainty 58
- Changing your worry thinking 60
  - How are our thoughts affected? 60
  - Core beliefs 61
  - Cognitive errors 61
  - Why do we think in unhelpful ways? 73
  - Underlying assumptions of logical errors 75
  - Understanding automatic thoughts 77
  - Catching automatic thoughts 78
  - Understanding and noticing logical errors 80
  - Reframing your thoughts (cognitive restructuring) 82
  - Making the restructured thinking habitual 86
  - Targeting the assumptions 86
- Some final points 90
- Additional reading 91

Introduction

Do you worry about everything? Do you overly analyse what you are thinking and doing or what other people are doing or might be thinking? Are you consistently searching for answers to the questions you have about the uncertainty of life? If you are, it sounds exhausting. The problem is that you end up tying yourself in knots worrying about an uncertain future, the intentions of others, or the risks you face. You go through life carrying a feeling that something bad could happen at any time. Yes, it definitely sounds exhausting.

Worry is associated with a constant state of anxious arousal with waves of even more intense anxiety states in between. Even though it is unpleasant to feel this way, it is very hard to stop worrying, even when you try hard just to make it stop. This workbook is designed to help you gain some control over this tendency you have to worry all the time.

What you need to know about worry

Worry occurs when you go over and over something in your mind without any effective outcome. Although worry may cause you to feel like you are doing something useful, that is, preparing you for things that may happen in the future, it does little to prepare you for anything.

Worry does not change the past and does not affect the future. All it does is make your present very uncomfortable and unpleasant. It certainly does not help you prepare to deal with things that might happen. It is not productive in this way. When you worry, you are not engaging in a problem-solving process that would help you to deal with a situation you are facing. It is not that sort of thinking. Rather than helping you prepare for the future, it is more like running on the spot… you never get anywhere.

If worry was useful as a problem-solving process, it would stop when you work out an effective plan to solve a problem you face. However, that is not what occurs. Even if you are worrying about a known problem, there is no end to the worry and unpleasant feelings of anxiety as it would if you were engaging in a process that was effective in some way.

The same can be said about over-analysing things. There is never an answer to the endless questions you have about the meaning behind the things that consume your thoughts. Really, there is fundamentally no difference between worrying and over-analysing.

The features of worry

There are some features of worry that make it problematic. These features also make worry different from other types of thinking, including a process of problem-solving. Let's consider these features here.

Catastrophising

Worrying thoughts typically relate to the prediction of a catastrophe in the future as the possible outcome of the thing you are worrying about. Your attention is on potential extreme and threatening outcomes of events that may occur. Your focus is on the worst-case scenario.

> *Anna was worried about making mistakes at work. She ruminated about what would happen if she made a mistake. She convinced herself that she would lose her job if she made the smallest of mistakes. She thought about what would happen if this occurred, so she worried that she would lose her home and have nowhere to live because of her changed financial circumstances. Everything she did at work would trigger this torment, worrying about making a mistake.*

Increased anxiety

Worrying increases feelings of anxiety or tension. You experience nervousness and upset with a general sense that something bad is going to happen.

> *As a result of Anna catastrophising about homelessness as a result of making even the tiniest of mistakes at work, she experienced significant anxiety symptoms. Her heart would race, and she felt tense and upset. When dealing with work tasks, her hands would shake, and her breathing would be fast and shallow. These symptoms were very unpleasant, but there seemed to be nothing Anna could do about them.*

Inability to tolerate uncertainty

Worrying is associated with being unable to deal with uncertainty about the future. Energy is spent trying to ensure that the catastrophes you think could happen will not happen.

> *As a result of being worried about losing her home and being homeless, because she made a mistake at work, Anna would repeatedly go over work she had already done to check it for errors. She couldn't just leave it to chance. She had to check everything. She thought this was the best way to prevent being fired and the financial catastrophe that would occur as a consequence. Of course, this caused her productivity to diminish. Anna worried about this, too.*

Problems accepting risk

An inability to accept risk means that extreme efforts are made to ensure that nothing bad happens in the future or that all attempts are made to prevent anything bad from occurring.

> *Anna could just not take the risk of losing everything because of a silly mistake. She would stay back late at work to make up for the time it would take her to repeatedly check her work for errors. She wouldn't spend any money, even on important things, because she wanted to have some savings in case she was fired. She did everything she could to minimise the risk of her ultimate concern of being homeless.*

Unsuccessful problem solving

All efforts are made to find a problem-resolution plan for the predicted catastrophe you envision. However, no matter what plan you set in place, the potential of successful resolution never seems attainable. In this way, no plan is good enough.

> *Despite all her efforts to ensure she was not fired from her job and that she would not be made homeless, Anna was never satisfied that she had done enough to ensure catastrophes didn't happen. She thought her work practises were insufficient to protect her from being fired. Whatever way she looked at it, and no matter how hard she worked or how much money she saved, she still believed that the outcome would be the same, that is, she would end up homeless.*

Trying to achieve perfection

With the goal of trying to feel secure and safe, attempts are made to find the 'perfect' solution to the problem you anticipate happening.

> *Anna set out to come up with the perfect way of handling her concerns so that she could relax and feel secure about her future. She stayed at work later and later going over various plans to ensure no mistakes were made. She discarded various strategies she came up with because she could always see ways they would not work. She thought there must be a solution to her problem, but she couldn't see what that solution might be.*

Unhelpful beliefs related to worry

There are unhelpful and unrealistic beliefs about the effectiveness of worry that end up contributing to worry. These beliefs relate to features of worry such as a sense of exaggerated threat, a feeling of helplessness in terms of the ability to cope with the predicted future event, an inability to deal with not knowing how things will turn out, and the belief that worrying actually helps.

> *Notwithstanding the fact that Anna knew others could make a mistake and not lose their job, Anna felt that it was likely to happen to her. She thought that if she lost her job she just wouldn't be able to cope and wouldn't know what to do to protect herself from the ultimate negative outcome of homelessness. She thought that worrying would help solve her problems.*

Failure to control worry

Repeated attempts are made to stop worrying. However, they all fail. In fact, in many cases, the strategies chosen increase worry rather than eliminate it.

> *Anna knew she was worrying too much. It was not that she did not try to control her worry. In fact, she told herself she was being silly and that it was unlikely that she would be fired for making an error in her work. She knew that other people made mistakes and did not get fired. She tried to distract herself and relax. Nothing worked. Indeed, the more she told herself that she should not worry because it was unlikely that she would be fired, the more she worried. She felt that the moment she let go of the worry would be the very time she would make the one mistake that would lead to her loss of employment and loss of her home.*

Worrying about worrying

This refers to worrying about being unable to stop worrying. You worry because you are worrying.

> *Anna was anxious and exhausted. She knew her worrying was creating problems for her, but she knew she couldn't stop. Her worrying was making her feel so bad that she was worried. She was worried that her worrying was not going to be effective.*

So, there are a number of features of worrying thoughts that make them different from other types of thoughts. These features tend to be apparent when the worry process is triggered. They do not tell you what you worry about but do reflect the way you worry.

The things you worry about

There are a multitude of things people worry about. Worry starts as an intrusive thought that gains your attention. These thoughts tend to be focused on the future ('what if' thoughts), although we can spend time thinking about the past ('if only' thoughts). Both can be anxiety-provoking. The 'what if' thoughts typically focus on potential future threats or negative outcomes.

We all have many thoughts popping into our minds every day. Most of these thoughts we can ignore. However, for someone who is prone to worrying, there are some types of thoughts that trigger the worry process. These thoughts have particular characteristics.

> *A high degree of personal importance or relevance:* The thoughts that get your attention are those that relate to your aims in life, your values and the things that matter to you.

> *An exaggerated sense of threat:* Worry thoughts tend to be those that are associated with a perception of a negative outcome, especially an extremely negative outcome. This perceived threat can relate to you or someone you care about.

> *Associations with a particular trigger:* Something will happen that acts like a reminder for you to be worried. This might be in the form of a strong association (e.g., you see an aeroplane overhead and you think about your partner travelling for business, so you start to worry about your partner being in a plane crash the next time they go on a business trip) or in the form of a weaker association (e.g., you glance at an article in the newspaper about fundraising efforts for an organisation and you think about the cost of living so you start to worry about how you will survive financially after you retire).

So, you now understand a bit more about the nature of what you worry about. These features make what you worry about problematic. But is all worry bad?

Differences between good and bad worry

One way to consider worry is in terms of what it is actually able to achieve, and not just what you hope it helps you achieve but is unlikely to do so. So, good worry is productive and bad worry is unproductive. Let's consider the differences between the two. We will do this by considering what you are doing and comparing that with what you could do instead.

Table 1: The alternatives to bad worry.

What you are doing	*What you could do instead*
Worrying about things that *might* happen in the future.	Think about immediate, real problems that you can solve.
Relentlessly chasing feelings of safety and certainty in relation to the thing you are worrying about.	Be open to tolerating a certain level of risk and uncertainty.
Worrying about things you imagine might be a problem over which you have no control.	Expend your energy dealing with problems that are coming up over which you do have some control or can influence in some way.
Rejecting all the possible ways you could solve a problem you are worried about because none of them is guaranteed to be successful.	Try out potential problem solutions to see how effective they might be.
Worrying about how stressed you would be if the thing you are worried about actually happened.	Think of ways to solve the problem usefully if it ever happens.
Always thinking about the worst-case scenario.	Adopt a more balanced approach, looking at all aspects of the thing you are worrying about, including the positive and neutral aspects – not just the negative aspects.
Always feeling like you are unable to cope with the thing you are worried about.	Develop more self-confidence about your ability to cope.
Experiencing severe anxiety.	Experience low levels of anxiety.

As you can see, there are alternatives to worry. In particular, it seems that the major difference is that worrying is unproductive, whereas adopting a genuine problem-solving approach is productive.

What is the difference between worrying and problem-solving?

Worry is the endless rumination, usually about things that might happen in the future (or may not). It is a relentless and endless cycle of thoughts, usually of a catastrophic nature. That is, you tend to think in a way that generates ideas about terrible things that could happen or the worst-case scenario. There is always something to worry about. If it is not one thing, it is another. You tell yourself that you are preparing yourself to solve the problems you might face, but that is not what is happening. It is associated with a generalised anxiety state and no amount of worrying thought will make it go away. Consider this example.

> *Judith and her young daughter had been staying with Judith's mother after a period of ill health. Judith's doctors told her she had recovered and she could just get on with things. Judith knew it was time to return home, but she feared she would not cope with the demands of looking after her home and caring for her child. She fully expected that things were going to fall apart as she wouldn't be able to cope alone. No amount of reassurance could change her point of view. She felt anxious and fearful of the outcome of her return to her life. This had not really been triggered by her ill health. She had always been a worrier and always tended to look to the future with pessimism. She just assumed that things would not turn out well. She hated feeling like this, but she found that she just kept going over and over her concerns without finding a way to calm her anxiety about what was going to happen.*

In contrast, problem-solving is a specific process focused on known or identifiable problems. As part of this process, you generate possible solutions to a specific problem, consider the likelihood of any of these solutions being effective, and then select the potential solution that is likely to work the best. Then, knowing what you are going to do, you either go ahead and engage in your problem-solving solution or you let the matter go, knowing that you are prepared for when the problem arises. Consider this example.

> *Judith and her young daughter had been staying with Judith's mother after a period of ill health. It was time for Judith to return home and pick up her life. Her doctors had assured her that she was fine with doing this. Judith was concerned about how she was going to cope. In the face of this concern, Judith thought about possible ways she could deal with any problems that might arise. On the one hand, Judith thought she could arrange for some family support at home to help her deal with settling back in. She thought she could get her mother and sister to visit her regularly. She thought she could ask for any further assistance from them if the need arose. On the other hand, Judith thought another way of handling this would be to alternate between time spent at her own home and time spent at her mother's home until she felt confident enough to manage things herself at home. Judith considered these options. She thought that the latter option*

> *would be too disruptive for her daughter, having to go back and forth between their home and Judith's mother's home. So, Judith decided to go with her first idea and make arrangements for some help from her family members as she transitions back to her home and life. She felt reassured by this decision and went about making the arrangements.*

It is clear that worry is linked with a generalised anxiety state that is unrelenting in nature. The process of worry does not alleviate your anxiety. In contrast, a problem-solving process may be associated with feelings of apprehension until such time as you select and apply your problem-solving approach, at which time your feelings of apprehension disappear.

The link between worry and Generalised Anxiety Disorder

Worrying thoughts have been associated with a range of psychological conditions. However, they are most commonly related to a condition called Generalised Anxiety Disorder. Among other diagnostic criteria outlined in the Diagnostic and Statistical Manual of Mental Disorders, 5th edition (DSM-5), to be diagnosed with Generalised Anxiety Disorder, you must experience three or more of the following symptoms for at least six months:

    Restlessness or feeling keyed up or on edge

    Being easily fatigued

    Difficulty concentrating or mind going blank

    Irritability

    Muscle tension

    Sleep disturbance (difficulty falling or staying asleep, or restless unsatisfying sleep).

You can see that a worried state of mind can be associated with these types of symptoms. Given that there is an integral relationship between worrying and anxiety, it is worthwhile to learn more about anxiety states.

What you need to know about anxiety

It is important to understand your anxiety reactions as they are linked so strongly to worrying thoughts. You may know that you feel anxious, but you may not yet understand what is happening to you when you are feeling anxious. This can make your anxiety reactions more disturbing than they need to be. So, let's consider how your nervous system works.

What is my nervous system doing?

Your autonomic nervous system (ANS) is the part of your nervous system that drives your functioning. It regulates your heart rate and temperature and makes other adjustments that are required for you to function on a moment-by-moment basis.

Your ANS is divided into two parts: the parasympathetic nervous system and the sympathetic nervous system. Your parasympathetic nervous system is the part of your ANS that should be driving you most of the time. It makes sure everything is ticking along so that your body gets what it needs, and you can function well.

Your sympathetic nervous system has a specialised function. It is your self-protection system that automatically activates when you are under threat. So, if you were crossing the road and a truck came screaming around the corner, your sympathetic nervous system would activate so that you could quickly and efficiently move out of the way of the truck and reach safety. Adrenaline would release into your system, causing your hands to shake and your heart rate to increase, but you would reach the safety of the footpath on the other side of the road, and you would be fine. Your brain would then recognise that you were safe, and your sympathetic nervous system would turn off, and your parasympathetic nervous system would take over again.

Your sympathetic nervous system is attuned to your brain perceiving signs of threat. It activates when you are at risk of harm and prepares you to deal with that threat. It is an effective self-protection system when you are under threat. Unfortunately, for people who develop overly sensitive sympathetic nervous systems or for people who continuously worry, their sympathetic nervous system will activate at the slightest indication that something is wrong and will prepare them to deal with the threat. This can occur even when there really is no threat to manage. This is what happens when you are anxious in the absence of an obvious cause of your anxiety, and this is the case when you are worrying. In effect, your brain cannot distinguish between an external threat (e.g., a truck coming around the corner) and an internal threat (e.g., you thinking worrying or anxiety-provoking thoughts). An overly sensitive nervous system will rely on its self-defence mechanism to protect you from perceived harm.

Your nervous system will also react to crises in your life that do not present the same level of physical harm. Although it is stressful to be worrying all the time, this itself is not physically threatening to you. Nevertheless, your sympathetic nervous system can be triggered by your worrying thoughts. As stated, your brain cannot always distinguish between an external threat to your physical integrity and an internally generated reaction to the threat to your emotional well-being.

Below is a table providing an overview of the activities of the parasympathetic and sympathetic nervous systems.

Table 2: The functions of the parasympathetic and sympathetic nervous systems.

	Parasympathetic	Sympathetic
Eyes	Constricts pupils	Dilates pupils
Salivary glands	Stimulates salivation	Inhibits salivation
Heart	Slows heartbeat	Accelerates heartbeat
Lungs	Constricts bronchi	Dilates bronchi
Stomach	Stimulates digestion	Inhibits digestion
Liver	Stimulates bile release	Simulates glucose release
Kidneys		Stimulates release of adrenaline and noradrenaline*
Intestines	Stimulates peristalsis and secretion	Inhibits peristalsis and secretion
Bladder	Contracts bladder	Relaxes bladder

* Also known as epinephrine and norepinephrine

When your sympathetic nervous system is activated, a series of physical changes occur that make sense if they are in response to a threat to your physical integrity. Some of these changes are listed below.

>Adrenaline is released so that you are alert and in a heightened state, ready to deal with the threat. This causes your heart rate to increase and can cause your hands, or even your whole body, to shake.

>Your hearing and your eyesight become better than normal. Everything sounds louder than it really is, and it is difficult to tolerate lots of light and movement. This is why anxious people tend to avoid places like supermarkets. Too much noise, too

much light, and too much movement can be overwhelming when you feel anxious. Anxious people tend to tolerate these things poorly because of the acuteness of their senses when their sympathetic nervous systems are activated. It helps to have really good hearing and eyesight if you are being threatened, but it does not help if you are just trying to do some shopping.

In our view, the most amazing thing that happens is that your sympathetic nervous system shuts down the systems it does not need to be using. For example, when under threat, your body needs to produce lots of glucose for energy, so it stimulates glucose production. In a high arousal state, you burn through that glucose quickly. Other systems that are not needed are shut down so that more energy is available for dealing with threat. In particular, your sympathetic nervous system shuts down your gastrointestinal system (e.g., inhibits digestion and inhibits peristalsis and secretion, with peristalsis referring to the contraction of the muscles that push forward the contents of your digestive tract). This is all right if it is shut down for the period of time it takes for you to deal with a truck coming around the corner. Your body copes less well with your gastrointestinal system not functioning well if the sympathetic nervous system activation is prolonged. You can lose your appetite, experience nausea, develop diarrhoea or constipation, and you can experience difficulty eating, or you will overeat to try to control the uncomfortable state of your digestive system.

All of these symptoms make sense if you are under threat but become a problem if the activation of your sympathetic nervous system is prolonged. Also, when your sympathetic nervous system is activated for reasons other than obvious threat, you can develop a sense of imminent danger just because your sympathetic nervous system has taken over your functioning. When your sympathetic nervous system is activated, your brain will interpret this as a sign that something is wrong. This explains why you feel this overwhelming sense that something terrible is going to happen that increases your worry.

Later, we will introduce you to some straightforward ways you can bring your sympathetic nervous system under better control so your anxiety and fear are reduced. You can learn to control the messages being received because you are worried so that the message is not misinterpreted, and you can avoid the sense that something terrible is going to happen.

Range of arousal

To understand how things work, you should be aware that human beings have a range of nervous system arousal within which we function the best. This range is quite large, from low in the range when we are very relaxed to high in the range when our nervous system is most 'revved up'. Pictured below is a diagram of this arousal range. The range within which you function best is known as the *window of tolerance*.

Within this window of tolerance, you have the flexibility to respond to the demands being placed on you. In this way, your arousal level will increase when you are faced with a demand and then decrease when that demand is over. As long as your arousal stays within this window, you will respond well to pressures placed on you.

If your arousal level drops below the lowest point of that range, you will enter a state of hypoarousal. In this state, you will feel slowed down and lethargic. Your functioning at this point will be inadequate, and your ability to respond to demands will be poor. If your arousal increases beyond the ceiling level, you will enter a state of hyperarousal. When this occurs, you can feel too aroused and can feel anxious and panicky. Your functioning will be impacted, and your ability to cope with pressures will deteriorate.

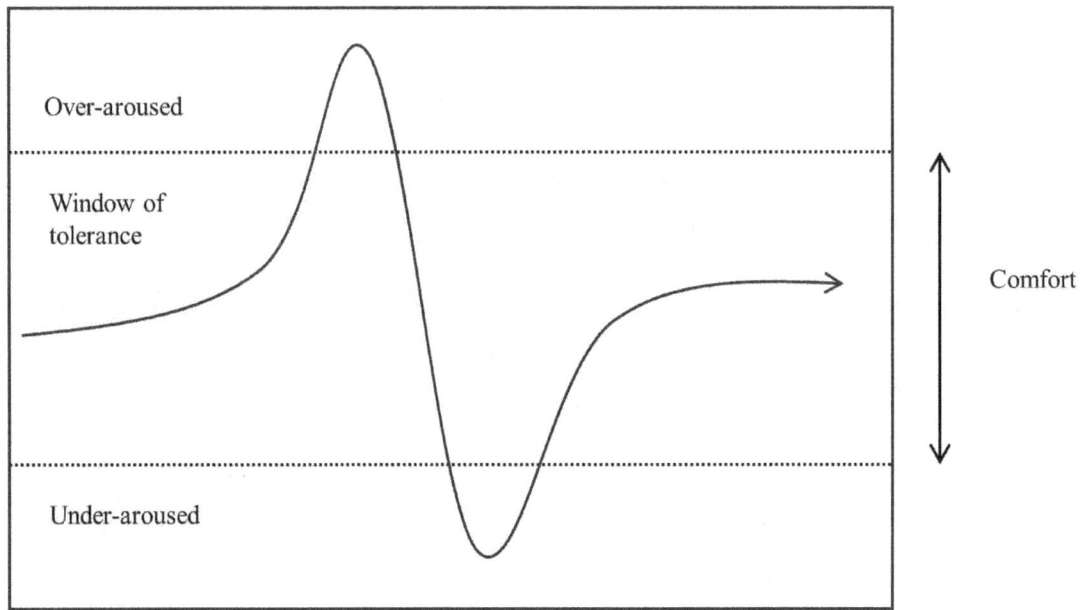

Figure 1: A diagram of the window of tolerance.

When you have been worrying about too much for too long, your arousal level creeps up from an optimal level of arousal in the middle of the window of tolerance to the upper extremes. You will find that you cannot or do not reduce that high level of arousal, even when you should be able to let go. This is why people cannot sleep well when they are under pressure. They can never relax enough for their arousal to decrease to a comfortable state. So, your 'baseline' arousal level, which is the starting point from which you respond to life demands, is high up in the range instead of midway.

So, your arousal level remains elevated. You barely notice this because it starts to feel normal to be under that much stress with your arousal level that high. But a problem exists. When any other thing occurs to which you have to respond or your level of worry increases, your arousal level will increase to deal with that additional demand being placed on you. However, the starting point of your arousal level, or your baseline arousal level, is already so high that you have no room to move. Any increase in arousal will push you through the ceiling and into an uncomfortable and unpleasant hyperaroused state. You will experience intense anxiety as a result.

Your high starting point gives you no flexibility to respond to even minor additional stressors or an increase in worry. So, the ways you normally cope with demanding situations fail because you have moved out of the range where you can successfully apply your usual coping strategies.

Your goal should be to get your nervous system back under control. Having too many demands placed on you has pushed your arousal level to the upper limits of your window of tolerance. Extra demands, even minor ones, then cause your arousal level to move beyond the ceiling of the window of tolerance and uncomfortable and unpleasant anxiety symptoms are then experienced.

You need to aim to bring your optimal arousal level down to at least the middle of the window of tolerance, with a baseline or starting point, when you are at your most relaxed, to the lower end of that range. Remembering that it now feels almost normal to have your nervous system so 'revved up', you need to retrain your nervous system to have a better starting point and a better optimal arousal level.

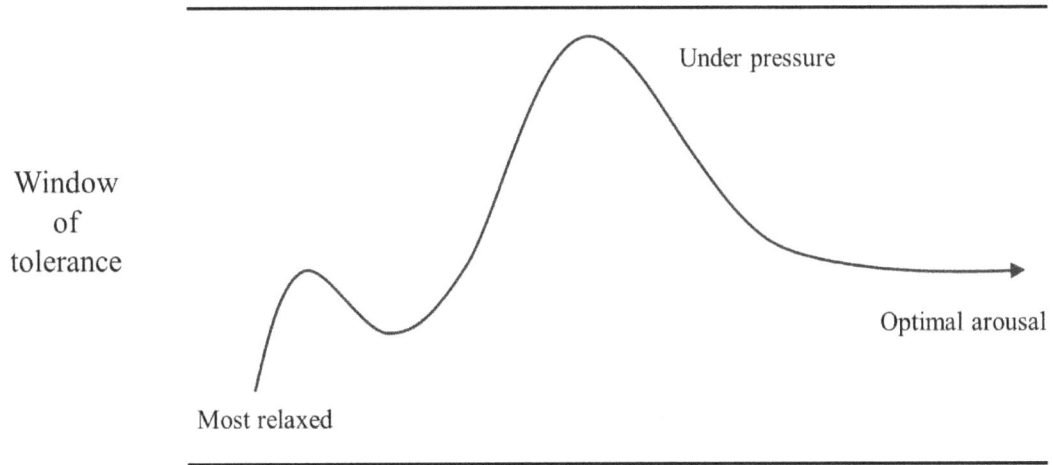

Figure 2: A diagram of an optimal level of arousal.

We will teach you ways to manage your anxiety response and keep your nervous system arousal within the window of tolerance later in this workbook. Before we do that, there are some things you need to consider one other manifestation of generalised anxiety that reflects the constant worry you experience. We are referring to the problems that occur with your attention and concentration.

The problem of attention and concentration

One problem that is reported regularly by people who are in an anxious state is that their attention and concentration has been affected. This is also true for people who have been overwhelmed by a tendency to worry.

We know that problems of attention and concentration occur with particular conditions, such as Attention Deficit Hyperactivity Disorder and Generalised Anxiety Disorder. However, excessive worry can produce the same problems for people. Remember, excessive worry can push your nervous system arousal up towards the top of your window of tolerance. It is at this point that you start to notice these types of difficulties.

How these problems manifest

There are lots of ways in which these problems manifest. At first, you would probably notice difficulty remembering things. Lots of people attribute the problems of attention and concentration to memory deficits and they start to worry there is something wrong with their memory. Below are some examples of the ways in which problems of attention and concentration appear.

What was I saying?

You might forget what you were about to say. You will be halfway through a sentence and you forget what you were planning to say next. You can start to give an account of an experience and then fail to recall the end of the story, even though it is something known to you. Although everyone experiences these problems from time to time, it is the frequency with which they occur when you are worrying that can disturb you.

Losing track

You might lose track of what you are reading or programmes you are watching on television. This is a common complaint. Overly stressed people will start reading and, even though they continue to read, they realise they cannot recall what they just read and will have to start again. This is particularly problematic for people who have to read things as part of their job or who read as a form of relaxation. The same thing can happen when watching a programme. The point or plot of what you are watching is lost.

What was I doing?

You might lose track of what you are doing or where you were going and what you intended to do when you got there. This can be frustrating. You might walk into a room with seemingly clear intention to do something, but them become completely confused about why you went into the room in the first instance. People with problems of attention and concentration will report going into a shop to buy a couple of items but leave without those items because they could not recall what they intended to buy so they bought something else instead. This manifestation of the problem can cause you to waste time having to backtrack to try to remember what it was you were doing or revisit places you have already been where you failed to do what you set out to do.

Making mistakes

These problems of attention and concentration can cause you to make mistakes that you would not normally make. You lose track of what you are doing and fail to notice that you have missed something or entered the wrong information or made some other simple error. Sometimes, these simple errors can set off a series of ongoing errors that end up creating a bigger problem than making a simple error would suggest would occur. To overcome the problem, people will either slow down or check and re-check what they have done. These are time consuming activities that further burden you when you are already worried enough.

Causes of the problem

The simple answer to why you are having problems with attention and concentration is that you are too stressed and your arousal level is too high. However, this does not really tell you what it is about being too stressed or too aroused that results in attention and concentration difficulties. We need to break it down to consider the individual factors that impact on the development of these problems.

Cognitive load

Firstly, the problems of attention and centration and, therefore, memory, occur because of the cognitive load being experienced by your brain. Fundamentally, you have too many things to worry about at once and your brain tries to give them all some attention. This reduces how much attention can be directed to any one thing. Even when you try to concentrate on one thing, your brain still recognises that there are lots of other things on your mind and checks to make sure that there is nothing that needs to be attended to with these other things.

Intrusive thoughts

The issue with cognitive load then causes you to experience intrusive thoughts about things that are not currently of central concern to you. With your brain trying to keep track of everything that is going on, you will be distracted by 'reminder' thoughts that are a reflection of the fact that your brain has focused briefly on one of the other multitude of things you have to worry about. These types of thoughts enter your mind in one of two ways. They either briefly appear but are enough to interfere with your concentration on what you are currently doing. Alternatively, the intrusion of the 'reminder' thought can distract you and your concentration on the thing you are currently doing is lost.

Attentional bias

Your brain has what is known as attentional bias. That is, it pays attention to the things that are most important to your survival. With a survival bias, your brain may draw your attention to things that seem particularly stressful or cause you to focus on how you are feeling rather than on what you need to be doing. With a survival bias, most of your attention will not be devoted to things such as the demands of your job or your home life. A survival bias allows your brain to recognise that there are indicators that you are stressed and to focus on the things you most need to be aware of in a crisis. These things are not the shopping list or the spreadsheet you might be working on in your job or the book you are reading.

Executive functioning

Executive functioning is the term used to describe the processes that take place in your brain that help you plan, organise and set goals and work towards them. The various components of your executive functioning include (a) planning and organisation (prioritising tasks, setting goals, and organising materials); (b) working memory (holding information and manipulating it in your mind); (c) inhibition (controlling impulses and controlling thoughts and actions); (d) attention (focusing of specific things and shifting attention from one thing to another); and (e) cognitive flexibility (easily adapting to changing circumstances and the ability to adjust plans).

Worry, and the anxiety it triggers, has the following influences on your executive functioning. It reduces *attentional control* making it hard to filter out things that can distract you. This causes you to have trouble concentrating. It causes you to *overestimate threat.* In this way, you perceive situations as more threatening or dangerous than is actually the case. It causes you to experience difficulty in *goal-oriented behaviour.* When stressed, you will find it harder to set goals and pursue them in an effective manner. The effect of stress on your executive functioning *impairs decision-making.* It is harder to decide what to do so the quality of your decision-making is poorer than it would be otherwise. It has an influence on *self-regulation.* It is hard to keep a good control of your emotional state, your thoughts and your actions.

All of these influences make it harder for you to attend to what you are doing and concentrate on the things that need your attention. It can make you feel less capable and more uncertain.

How can I fix this?

The good news is that the same strategies that are used to manage your nervous system arousal will resolve the problems of attention and concentration. We will be looking at these strategies later in this workbook.

Is it safe to stop worrying?

It feels like worry fulfils a useful purpose. It feels like worry is preparing you for an uncertain future. As a result, it can feel like giving up worrying is an unsafe thing to do. In some strange and unusual ways, you can think that bad things will happen if you do not pay attention, so it is better to worry about them in advance. This gives worry some sort of magical properties. Instead of just making you more anxious in the present, you can believe that it protects you in the future.

None of this is true. Worry just makes things more unpleasant in the present. It is safe to stop worrying. You would be better off learning to effectively problem-solve and then have confidence in your ability to do so if you are actually faced with a problem in the future.

How can I stop worrying?

We are going to cover a variety of methods to stop worrying. These approaches are outlined here.

> We are going to start with learning to manage your anxiety symptoms. Learning anxiety control is a fundamental part of learning to stop worrying. It will help resolve any problems with attention and concentration.
>
> We will then move to focusing on worry itself. To begin this process, we will introduce some worry control strategies that can help immediately to start to bring your worry under control.
>
> We will then provide you with some information about sleep disturbance and how you can control the worrying thoughts that tend to keep you awake at night.
>
> We will then introduce a worry decision tree that will help to introduce the notion that you can choose to think differently and act differently than the way your worry is pushing you.
>
> Building on this, we can then consider a process of how to change bad worry into more effective problem-solving.
>
> We will then consider how to manage a particular feature of worry that is problematic, that is, the inability to tolerate uncertainty. We will introduce ways to challenge uncertainty and learn to tolerate it.
>
> From challenging uncertainty, we will then focus on learning to challenge other types of thinking that impact worry and teach you ways to replace that thinking with more realistic and effective thinking.

How to combat anxiety

How do you achieve anxiety management? Consider the following. When you are in an elevated or heightened state, at the top of your window of tolerance or beyond it, your heart rate increases and your breathing changes. Your heart rate elevation is caused by a release of adrenaline that occurs when your sympathetic nervous system is triggered. This can be very uncomfortable, and it feels like there is very little you can do about it.

Your breathing changes contribute to the elevation in your heart rate. When people are stressed, their breathing tends to be rapid and shallow. You can liken this pattern of breathing to the waves on top of the water. Form a picture in your mind of the way a child draws waves. When we are stressed, we tend to breathe in sharply, then breathe out quickly and then breathe in again quickly. You tend not to breathe all the way out before you breathe in again. This inhalation-exhalation pattern is what affects your heart rate.

In contrast, when you are relaxed, your breathing tends to be deeper and slower and has a pattern that is similar to the swell in the ocean. The inhalation-exhalation pattern is a comfortable breath-in followed by a long, slower breath-out. You do not breathe in again until you have breathed all the way out.

From the diagram below, you can see the pattern of anxious, rapid and shallow breathing on the top. Below that is the pattern of slower, deeper breathing that is characteristic of a more relaxed state.

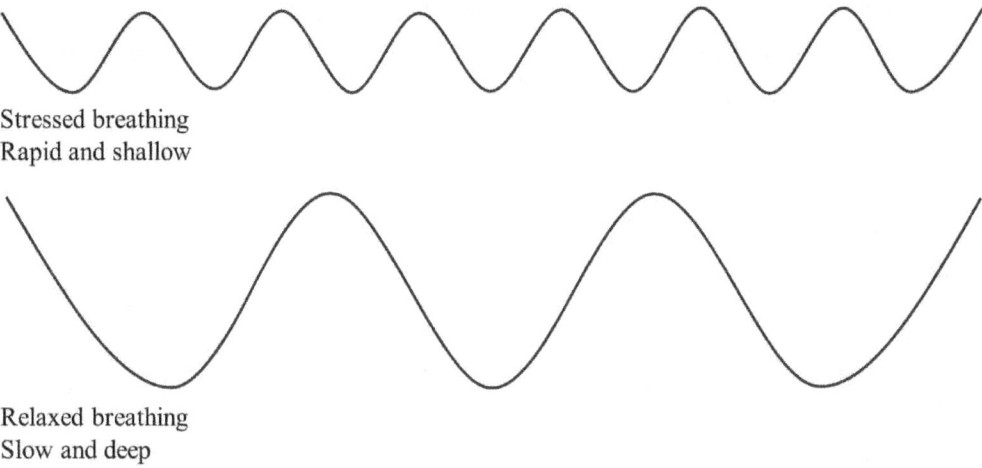

Figure 3: A comparison between stressed and relaxed breathing.

The reason your breathing pattern affects your heart rate is because these two things are linked. Under normal, stress-free conditions, your heart rate increases as you breathe in and then slows as you breathe out. This is normal. When you are stressed and your respiration rate increases and your breathing is shallower, your heart rate does not have a chance to slow before you breathe in again. Therefore, your heart rate is elevated and stays up.

Let's, for a moment, go back to the truck speeding around the corner, threatening to run you over. Your sympathetic nervous system is activated, allowing you to be in the right physical state to move quickly out of harm's way and protect yourself. When you get to the other side of the road, the truck goes past, and you are unharmed; your brain registers these experiences, your sympathetic nervous system turns off, and your parasympathetic nervous system takes over. This is because reaching the other side of the road and seeing the truck pass you by are safety signals. Your brain interprets these signs as indicators that you are going to be all right.

Of course, no such safety signals are available when you are in your loungeroom worrying about things. Worrying is not the sort of event that allows for a safety signal. Your brain would struggle to identify safety indicators because they do not exist in that sort of form. What you can do is offer your brain a safety signal but of a different type.

You can send a message that everything is all right by deliberately slowing your heart rate from its elevated rate to a more normal rate for you. Although it sounds difficult to achieve, controlling your heart rate is actually a reasonably straightforward undertaking. If you slow your breathing and lengthen your exhalation until you have breathed all the way out before breathing back in, your heart rate will come into line, and your heart rate will go down.

To use our waves and ocean swell analogy, the aim is to change the pattern of your breathing from waves on the top of the water to a pattern like the swell in the ocean, where the water is lifted up and then put back down as the swell passes. You are aiming for an easy, comfortable breath in, followed by a long, slow breath out.

The ideal situation is to breathe out for twice as long as it takes you to breathe in. Lengthening your breath out requires that you slow the amount of air you breathe out so that you can breathe out for longer. You should aim to breathe all the way out, emptying your lungs, before you gently and comfortably breathe back in.

This pattern of breathing should result in a slowed heart rate and a subsequent reduction in that sense of anxiety or crisis that occurs when your sympathetic nervous system is triggered. This occurs because your brain interprets the reduction in heart rate and the change in breathing pattern as a signal that the crisis is over.

Let's consider a simple exercise to control your breathing by deepening your breaths and slowing them down.

	Slowing and controlling your breathing
1.	Without trying to change your breathing, just notice for a moment the pattern of your inhalations and exhalations.
2.	Now, take a comfortable breath in. It does not have to be too deep, but rather just a comfortable breath.
3.	Now, breathe out, slowing the amount of air you exhale and lengthening your breath as a result.
4.	When your lungs feel empty of air, gently and comfortably breathe back in.
5.	As you breathe, practice lengthening your exhalation just a bit. You may also deepen your breath in slightly. Keep in mind the picture of the ocean swell if this helps.
6.	Practice this pattern of breathing for as long as you feel comfortable.

Exercise available at elemen.com.au

There is another element that you can add to this breathing exercise that may help with your ultimate goal of reducing your anxiety and signalling your sympathetic nervous system to turn off so your parasympathetic nervous system can do its job. You can include in this breathing exercise the element of reducing your muscle tension.

People who are stressed tend to have tense muscles. Although this muscle tension can occur anywhere in the body, common sites include the forehead and scalp, neck, jaw, shoulders, and chest. The increased muscle tension contributes to the overall sense of readiness to deal with threat. On the downside, tense muscles can cause headaches, chest and other pain.

If tense muscles present a significant problem for you, then a progressive muscle relaxation exercise may help. A general overview of this technique is provided below. More comprehensive versions are available online. However, another easy strategy is to link the relaxation of muscles with the breathing exercise.

As you breathe out, just relax your muscles in places where they feel tight and tense. You do not have to achieve marked muscle relaxation to experience a noticeable difference. Just drop your shoulders, relax your jaw, smooth your forehead or relax your stomach muscles. Aim for a gentle relaxation of tight muscles as you exhale.

The combination of breathing exercise and muscle relaxation can be used even when the focus is on controlling your breathing. You can also use the combined technique when your primary focus is on troubling muscle tension. In combination, the techniques can help with either target.

Combined breathing and muscle relaxation technique	
1.	Take a comfortable breath in. It does not have to be too deep, but rather just a comfortable breath.
2.	Now, breathe out, slowing the amount of air you exhale and lengthening your breath as a result. As you breathe out, drop your shoulders, relax your jaw, smooth your forehead and relax your abdominal muscles.
3.	When your lungs feel empty of air, gently and comfortably breathe back in.
4.	As you breathe, practice lengthening your exhalation just a bit. You may also deepen your breath in slightly. Keep in mind the picture of the ocean swell if this helps. Continue to relax your muscles slightly on each exhalation.
5.	Practice this pattern of breathing and muscle relaxation for as long as you feel comfortable.

Exercise available at elemen.com.au

As stated, if muscle tension presents you with a significant problem, you may wish to try a method of progressive muscle relaxation. This technique involves tensing your muscles and then relaxing them. Tensing your muscles before relaxing them has a number of purposes. It helps you to clearly identify where the tension in your body is located. It helps you feel the difference between a tense muscle and a relaxed one, which is helpful when the muscle has been tense for a long time. Finally, tensing the muscle first helps to induce deeper relaxation in that muscle when you relax it.

We will start with a longer version of the progressive muscle relaxation exercise that will help you learn the technique. You can then change to a shorter version that we describe below.

Progressive muscle relaxation (longer version)	
1.	Choose a comfortable place where it is quiet. Lay down or sit in a comfortable position with your feet flat on the floor.
2.	Now, clench both your fists… tighter and tighter. Notice the tension in your muscles. Keep it clenched for about 10 seconds. Now relax. Feel your muscles relax. Notice the difference between the tension and relaxation.
3.	Repeat the same procedure with your fists. Notice the difference between tension and relaxation.

4.	Now, bend your elbows on both arms and tense your biceps. Hold the tension. Now relax. Notice the difference between tension and relaxation.
5.	Repeat the same procedure with your elbows bent and your biceps tensed. Hold the tension, then relax. Pay attention to the change from tension to relaxation.
6.	Now, frown as hard as you can. Notice the tension in your forehead. Hold the tension. Now relax. Notice the difference you feel after you have released the tension.
7.	Now, frown again as hard as you can. Hold the tension, then release it. Notice the contrast between tension and relaxation.
8.	Now, close your eyes and squint them tightly. Hold the tension, then relax. Allow your eyes to feel a comfortable, relaxed state. Notice the change. Repeat by closing your eyes and squinting then relaxing, letting go of the tension.
9.	Now, clench your jaw. Bite down hard. Notice the tension throughout your jaw. Now, relax your jaw, allowing your teeth to fall apart slightly. Notice the feeling of relaxation. Repeat this exercise with your jaw.
10.	Now, press your tongue hard against the roof of your mouth. Hold it there. Feel the tension at the back of your mouth. Now relax. Notice the difference between the tension and relaxation. Repeat the exercise with your tongue.
11.	Now, purse your lips, pushing them out into an 'O' shape. Hold them there. Now, release the tension and relax. Notice how your mouth feels now that it is relaxed. Repeat the exercise with your lips.
12.	Now, press your head back as far as it will comfortably go. Hold onto the tension. Roll your head from the right to the left, allowing the focus of the tension to change. Now relax. Feel the difference between the tension in your neck and the relaxation. Repeat the exercise by pressing your head back.
13.	Now, bring your head forward with your chin on your chest. Feel the tension in your throat and the back of your neck. Hold the tension, then relax and allow your head to return to a comfortable position. Repeat the exercise by bringing your head forward.
14.	Now, shrug your shoulders, bringing your shoulders up and allowing your head to hunch down between them. Hold the tension. Now relax and notice the difference between tension and relaxation.

15.	Now, breathe in deeply and hold your breath. Hold it. Now, allow yourself to gently exhale, letting go of tension as you breathe out. Feel your body relax. Repeat the exercise, breathing in, then gently letting go.
16.	Now, tense your stomach muscles. Hold onto the tension. Now relax. Let your stomach muscles relax and appreciate that feeling. Repeat the exercise with your stomach muscles.
17.	Now, arch your back without straining. Hold onto the tension. Now, let it go. Notice the change in your muscles. Now repeat the exercise by arching your back.
18.	Now, tighten your buttocks and thighs. Press down on your heels to flex your thigh muscles. Hold onto the tension. Now relax and notice the difference. Repeat the exercise.
19.	Now, curl your toes downward to cause your calves to tense. Hold onto the tension. Now relax. Repeat the exercise.
20.	Now, draw your toes upward, causing your shins to feel tense. Pay attention to the tension. Now relax. Repeat the exercise.
21.	Now, scan your body. Notice if there are any tense spots. Repeat the exercise in that area.
22.	Enjoy the more relaxed feeling throughout your entire body. When you are ready, slowly return to your normal activities, holding on to that feeling of relaxation.

Exercise available at elemen.com.au

Once you have learned the technique, you can use a shorter version. You may prefer to just focus on the areas of your body that are particularly tense. It is certainly the case that some people tend to carry their muscle tension in one or two areas. Here is a shorter version that will allow you to tailor the procedure to suit your own needs.

	Relaxing using progressive muscle relaxation (short version)
1.	Choose a comfortable place where it is quiet. Lay down or sit in a comfortable position with your feet flat on the floor.
2.	Begin to work your way through groups of muscles by tensing them and relaxing them. For example, if you start with your forehead, tighten the muscles in your forehead by frowning. Hold for a few moments (10-15 seconds), then release, allowing the muscle in your forehead to relax, enjoying that experience for about 60 seconds. Notice the difference between the tension and the relaxation.
3.	Then, move on to the next group of muscles. You can work through groups of muscles from the top of your head to the tips of your toes, or you can select areas of your body that present a particular problem of tension for you.
4.	Repeat the process until you have worked your way through the groups of muscles you have selected.
5.	Repeat that process again, first tensing the muscles, holding that tension for five to ten seconds, and then relaxing those muscles.

Exercise available at elemen.com.au

So, controlling your breathing and, thus, lowering your heart rate will help you feel less anxious, as will reducing your muscle tension. It will also help you move to a better place in your window of tolerance. However, there are other approaches you can take to anxiety management.

More exercises to help

One of the problems with being anxious and 'revved up' is that your mind fills up with anxiety-provoking thoughts. This is the basis of worry. When you worry, you cannot seem to stop thinking in an endless stream of anxiety-provoking thoughts. This makes it very difficult to get your nervous system back under control. The thoughts racing through your mind do not allow you to relax. So, included here are some exercises that should help you settle your mind.

The first exercise aims to teach you to self-soothe. If you can learn to settle yourself, the racing thoughts in your mind may follow. The quieter your nervous system, the less active your mind is with anxiety-provoking thoughts.

What you are aiming to do is find ways to soothe yourself. Most of us can understand how we go about soothing an upset child. We might hold and rock a distressed child and say soothing things. What you are looking for are adult versions of self-soothing strategies that will help to alleviate your distressed state.

The goal of developing self-soothing strategies is to create for yourself some moments of less distress. The strategies are aimed at reducing your heightened state to a more manageable level. They allow your nervous system arousal level to be brought back under your control. So, strategies that allow you to focus on the here and now are the ones that will allow you to choose to be in a quieter state with a greater sense of peace of mind.

Consider the proposed self-soothing strategies listed below and select ones that you think might assist you. These may be things you have tried before or ones you feel might work for you. Some of these strategies require you to make an effort to seek out the means of engaging with them. However, others are using things that are readily available or easily obtained.

	Self-soothing strategies
	Take a shower or a warm bath. Focus your attention on the sensations created by the water. Enjoy the feeling of the water on your skin and the warmth of the water.
	Play with your pet, or just stroke your dog's or cat's coat. Interacting with your pet has been demonstrated to be soothing for many pet owners.
	Change into your most comfortable clothes. Enjoy the feel of the fabric and the degree of comfort you feel from wearing these items of clothing.
	Go for a swim. Enjoy the sensation of being in the water. Allow those sensations to quiet your mind. Even if you are not a good swimmer, bobbing around in the water can produce the same sensations.
	Treat yourself to a massage if that appeals to you. Allow your muscles to relax and your mind to quiet.
	Listen to soothing music. Allow your attention to be directed to the music rather than have the music in the background.
	Listen to an audiobook, even if your worry makes it difficult to concentrate. Try to pay attention to each word that is spoken. If you lose track of the story, you can always return to the previous track and pick up the story again.

	Turn on the television or talkback radio and engage in listening to what is being broadcast. The goal here is to focus your attention on the conversations as they play out rather than selecting a programme you are excited to watch or listen to. It is the process of listening to others talking that is soothing.
	Listen to the sounds of water running. Again, the aim is to listen to the sounds of the water, stopping your mind from going to other intrusive thoughts. You can find the sound of running water in various places. You can visit a naturally occurring water course or waterfall. You could listen to running water from an outdoor garden fountain. However, you can also get an indoor personal fountain that can be used at any time. Alternatively, you can listen to recorded sounds of water running.
	Find something soothing to look at. This might be by the water or an outdoor space such as a park. It could be photographs or paintings that you find soothing or relaxing. The goal is to find something to look at that is engaging for you and that you find relaxing and soothing.

Exercise available at elemen.com.au

Managing anxiety-related thoughts

Before considering ways to change your thinking from being focused on worrying thoughts, it is worth mentioning here some straightforward strategies for managing the sense of threat that anxious arousal causes. Although focusing on managing the physical manifestations of anxiety and focusing on quieting your nervous system can assist you, there is also value in quieting your anxious mind.

Simple threat reduction strategy

To start, there is a simple strategy that can help quiet a worried mind. People who worry live in a world where there is always something in the future to be concerned about. Too little attention is paid to the present. The anxiety you feel about the future destroys any peace of mind you might be able to have in the present.

Threat reduction strategy	
The strategy involves the following easy steps:	
1.	Catch yourself worrying.
2.	Evaluate your immediate environment for any signs of threat.
3.	Ask yourself if there is anything you need to do right now in relation to the thing you are worrying about.
4.	Give yourself permission to let go of your anxiety and worry.

Exercise available at elemen.com.au

Exercises in quieting your mind

There are strategies available for quieting your mind. Building on the notion of self-soothing, it is a good idea to be more present in your focus. If you give it some consideration, you will find that the thoughts racing through your mind when you are anxious typically are not related to what is happening in the here and now. Our thoughts tend to be time-travelling, that is, they are focused either on what has already happened or what is to come. They rarely focus on what is happening in the present moment when you are trying to relax and get your worry under control.

Usually, at these times, nothing is happening that is worth worrying about. If you could deliberately spend more time focused on the here and now and less time on the past or future, you would have a better chance of relaxing and quieting your overly stimulated nervous system.

The notion of focusing on the here and now is based on mindfulness techniques. Mindfulness refers to your ability to be aware of your emotions, your physical state, your actions and your thoughts in a state of mind that is absent from judgment or criticism of your experience. Research has demonstrated that mindfulness helps you to control symptoms of anxiety, to control the distress caused by particular situations, to increase your capacity to relax, and to learn how to cope better with challenging situations.

Based on the notion of mindfulness, we have included some exercises you can use to quiet your mind by focusing on the here and now. To do this well, you may need to practice the skill. When you first learn these techniques, it is easy to become distracted and return to your racing thoughts. Do not be concerned if this happens. Just return to your exercise and continue.

Mindful listening	
1.	Sit in a comfortable place, preferably by yourself. If you wish, close your eyes.
2.	Start to focus your attention on the sounds around you.
3.	Notice the changes in the sounds from moment to moment.
4.	Notice the times between sounds when it is quiet.
5.	Focus your attention both on what is happening inside and outside.
6.	Pay attention to the sounds and nothing else. Do not make judgments about the sounds. Just acknowledge the sound then listen to the next one.
7.	If thoughts about other things come into your mind, put them aside and then return to listening to the sounds around you.
8.	Do this for a few minutes or until you are ready to stop.

Exercise available at elemen.com.au

Let's try another mindfulness exercise.

Mindful use of your senses	
Sight	Look around you. Allow your attention to be drawn to five things in your immediate environment that you might not normally pay any attention to. For example, this might be the way the fruit is sitting in the fruit bowl, the way your curtain is hanging, or the way your books are placed on your bookcase. Allow your attention to rest on each of these things. Keep your focus directed at the item, setting aside any other thoughts that come into your mind.
Touch	Bring your attention to four things you can feel at this moment in time. For example, it may be the feel of the sun on your skin, or the feel of the fabric of your clothes against your skin, or the feel of the chair underneath you, or the feel of the table surface where your hand is resting. Allow your attention to rest on each of these feelings. Keep your focus directed at each sense of touch, setting aside any other thoughts that come into your mind.

Hearing	Listen to the sounds in your surroundings. Notice three things you can hear. For example, you might hear the sounds of cars travelling along the road, the noise of the refrigerator, or the sound of the wind in the trees. Focus your attention on each of these sounds. If other thoughts come into your mind, let those thoughts go and return to focusing on the sounds you can hear.
Smell	Pay attention and search for two things you can smell. For example, you might be able to smell whatever you are cooking, the scent of plants in your garden, or the sea air if you live near the water. Keep your attention focused on each of these smells. If other distracting thoughts come into your mind, let these thoughts go and return to focusing on the things you can smell.
Taste	When you are eating, focus your attention on the tastes you are experiencing. For example, take a sip of your coffee and notice the taste. Bite into your sandwich and notice the flavours. Really pay attention to the flavours of the things you are tasting. If you become distracted, let go of these interfering thoughts and return to focusing on the things you are tasting.

Exercise available at elemen.com.au

And there is one last mindfulness exercise.

	Mindful walking
1.	As you are ready for your walk, stand still for a moment. Sense the weight on your feet as you stand there. Feel how your muscles are supporting you and maintaining your stability and balance. Be aware of your arms in a comfortable position of your choice (e.g., by your side or hands clasped, either at the front or at your back). Allow yourself to stand there, relaxed but alert.
2.	Begin to walk. Choose a comfortable pace, not too fast and not too slow. Pay attention to how your feet and legs feel (e.g., their heaviness or lightness, energy, or even any pain). The way your legs and feet feel will form the focus of your attention. If you become distracted, return to focusing on your legs and feet.
3.	Pay attention to the way in which you lift your feet and place them back down on the surface on which you are walking. Notice how you lift your foot, swing your leg and place your foot down again ahead of where you were a moment before. Walk in a natural and relaxed manner. Move your arms in a way that feels normal for you.

4.	It is likely that your mind will wander as you walk along. Your attention will be drawn to what is around you or thoughts that come into your mind. Acknowledge that you have been distracted and return to focusing on the process of walking… the lifting of your foot, the swing of your leg and the placement of your foot in front of you. Just gently return your attention to the sensations of walking.
5.	You might focus on a point ahead of you. Focus on the steps you take as you move towards that point. One step at a time. Experience fully the sensations of walking.
6.	Keep walking mindfully until you reach your destination or the point where you decide to turn around and mindfully walk back to where you started.

Exercise available at elemen.com.au

These types of strategies can help deal with the anxiety that is linked with repeated worry. Next, we must consider how to control the worrying thoughts component of your problem.

How to combat worry

In addition to managing your anxiety symptoms, your efforts should also be directed toward managing your worry. We are going to combat your worry in a variety of ways. We will provide you with some worry control strategies based on what we know about the worry process. We will also apply a worry control strategy to your sleep problems if you experience them, explaining why sleep disturbance occurs. We will introduce you to the notion that you can choose to do things other than worry and that you can challenge the thoughts and assumptions you make that underlie your worry.

Worry control strategies

Let's begin. To understand how worry works, let's consider the simplified version of a worry model in the diagram below. You experience intrusive worry thoughts. These relate to possible future threats to yourself or others you care about. Then, a cycle of worry develops where you keep re-evaluating the threat, reaching the same conclusion that the threat is real or possibly real. No matter how many times you go over it, the threat continues to play on your mind. Of course, this causes you to feel anxious.

Here we are going to focus on some simple worry control strategies that will help you deal with your worrying by attempting to interrupt that cycle of worry. In effect, the cycle of worry causes you to feel anxious which causes you to worry more which causes you to feel more anxious. You need to step away from this cycle.

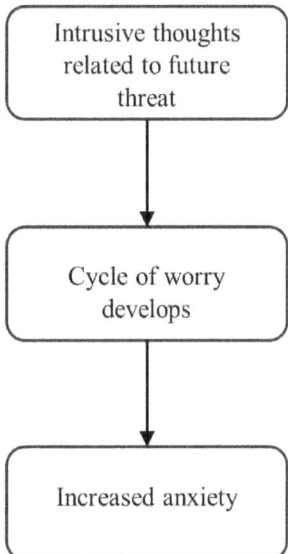

Figure 4: How a cycle of worry affects your anxiety.

The cycle of worry that develops is comprised of a number of different components. Consider the diagram below.

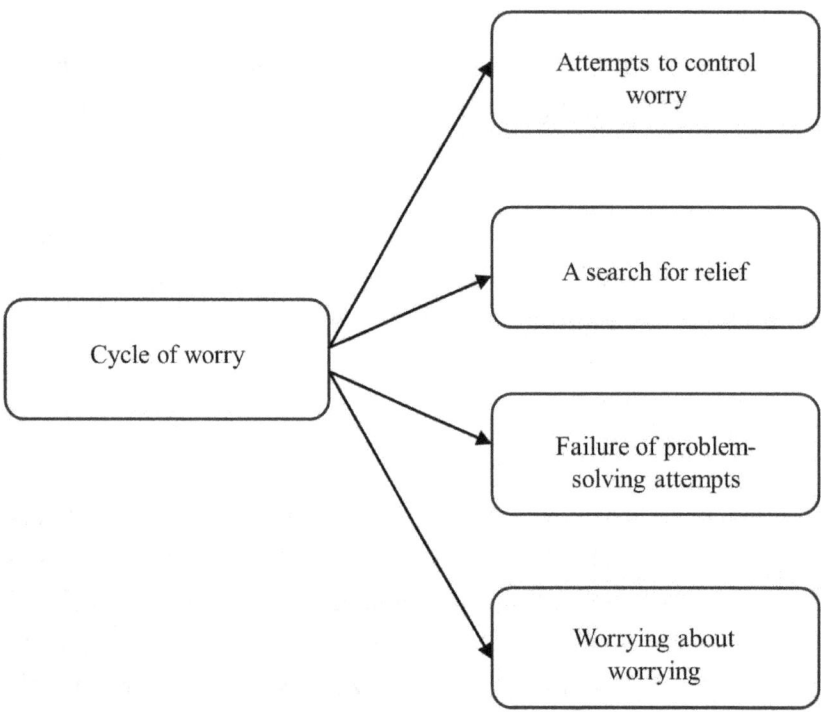

Figure 5: The components of the cycle of worry.

What happens in this cycle of worry? You make repeated attempts to control your worry despite the fact that you are aware that you cannot do this. That is the problem. If you could just stop worrying, you would. However, despite this knowledge that your worry is uncontrolled, you repeatedly try to control it nonetheless.

In fact, there are a number of things that you might use to control your worry that actually make it worse. These include:

Thought suppression: Telling yourself not to worry.

> A funny thing happens when you tell yourself not to think about something. That is, you tend to think about it more. So, telling yourself to stop worrying is not going to work.

Reassuring yourself: Telling yourself that things will be ok.

> If this is all it took, you would never worry. Of course, the problem is that you cannot be reassured. Nothing you say to yourself will make a difference. You will still question yourself, and you will still catastrophise about the future.

Seeking reassurance from others: Asking others to tell you things will be ok.

> In the same way that you cannot reassure yourself, seeking reassurance from others does not work to stop your worrying thoughts. No matter how genuine the efforts of other people might be, you will fail to accept the reassurance as being meaningful.

Checking: Repeatedly checking things to reassure yourself.

> Anyone with obsessive-compulsive disorder will tell you that checking to make sure everything is ok will not work to stop your worry and anxiety. In addition, it will not better prepare you for the catastrophe you anticipate. Further, the checking will not make you believe that you could handle the catastrophe if it occurred.

Self-criticism: Criticising yourself for worrying.

> Self-criticism never really fixes anything. Berating yourself for worrying will not stop you from worrying about the future. It will just make you feel worse.

Suppressing your emotion: Trying to push down your anxiety.

> Trying to keep your anxiety under control seems like a useful undertaking. However, suppressing the feeling means you are not actually doing anything to alleviate it. You are trying to fight your anxiety into submission. This will never work.

These things seem like useful strategies, but they are not. They do the opposite of what you intend. We will challenge the thinking behind these strategies later in this workbook.

Your efforts to control your worry will continue. This is because you feel anxious, which is unpleasant and uncomfortable. It is not surprising then that you search for some relief from those feelings. The trouble with this search is that nothing you do will stop the worry. This is because the things you are worrying about are things that you think might happen in the future. You know that you cannot really control the future, so you continue to worry and, therefore, feel anxious.

Remember what you learned about how your nervous system works. You are anxious when your sympathetic nervous system is activated for whatever reason. The assumption is made that because you feel anxious, something bad is going to happen. However, it is incorrect to assume that if all you do is reduce your anxiety, your worry will go away. It is wrong to expect that if you do not feel anxious, you will not have anything to worry about. Of course, if that were true, everyone would manage their anxiety and would never worry.

Because your worry persists and you continue to worry about that potential catastrophe in the future, and because your anxiety is telling you that you have something genuine to worry about, you look for ways to fix things.

Although it has been demonstrated that people who worry are able to solve their problems as well as people who do not worry, there are some features of their problem-solving that differ from non-worriers. In particular, worriers want an immediate solution to an anticipated problem even when they do not know when the problem will occur, if it will occur, and the nature of the problem if it does occur. It is this demand for an immediate solution that sets them apart from non-worriers who are more able to tolerate uncertainty and potential risk.

Also, in comparison with non-worriers, people who worry tend to have:

> Less confidence in their ability to resolve their problems.
>
> A tendency to be overly concerned about potential threats in the future.
>
> An expectation that things will not work out well, no matter how much they try to solve their problems.
>
> A need for a solution that is perfect and guaranteed to be effective for this potential problem in the future.
>
> A tendency to be focused on information that is not directly relevant to the problem they are anticipating.

These features cause people who worry to be ineffective in their problem-solving efforts. Rather than preparing for future problems, they end up 'running on the spot', repeatedly but unsuccessfully trying to solve problems that typically have not yet happened.

What happens is that you end up worrying about the fact you are worrying. You worry that you cannot control your worry and you worry about stopping worrying in case that increases the risk of a bad outcome. The fear about worrying causes you to try harder to control your worry using the same ineffective means.

All of this causes you to be stuck in a cycle of worry. You go over and over the same processes in a seemingly never-ending pattern. You need to act to break that cycle.

Interrupting the cycle

One way to interrupt that cycle of worry is to interrupt that pattern by distracting yourself with an alternative idea and managing your worry. In effect, the strategy helps break the habit of worrying. The strategy seems ridiculously simple but is often quite successful. Consider the following exercise.

	Allocating worry time
1.	Allocate a 15-minute period of your day for worrying. You choose the time that is more effective for you. For the purposes of this exercise, let's say you allocate 7.00-7.15 pm as your worry time.
2.	Throughout the day, catch yourself having worry thoughts. As soon as you notice you are worrying, acknowledge that you are worrying and tell yourself the following, "I will worry about that during my worry time, at 7.00 pm". Then, deliberately move your thoughts to something else.
3.	Do this as often as you catch yourself worrying. Do not be concerned that when you start doing this, you will probably catch yourself worrying many times. Just remember that each time you notice you are worrying, remind yourself that you will worry about it at your allocated time and then move on to thinking about something else.
4.	When your allocated time arrives, you have permission to worry as much as you like for 15 minutes. However, you do not have to do this. Most often, people will not be bothered. You may also find that it is actually quite difficult to deliberately worry for 15 minutes. That is ok. You do not have to worry if you do not want to.

Exercise available at elemen.com.au

Consider this to be the first step in controlling your worry. We will expand on this idea when we consider the worry decision tree later in this workbook. However, before we do that, it is worthwhile here to consider control of your worry when you are trying to sleep. Remember, when it is dark and quiet, and there is very little to distract you at night, your worry thoughts are likely to flood back. We need to think about a way to control this.

Dealing with sleep disturbance

One of the consequences of your nervous system being revved up and having too many worrying thoughts is that your sleep can become disturbed. You can become fatigued as a consequence and it becomes more difficult for you to cope with the demands of your day.

There are three types of insomnia. You might experience any one or all three of these types of sleep problems.

Trouble going to sleep. This is where you are unable to go to sleep despite being tired.

Trouble staying asleep. This is where you repeatedly wake throughout the night but, after a period of time, you are able to go back to sleep.

Waking early and being unable to go back to sleep. This is where you wake early in the morning, and despite needing more sleep, you cannot return to sleep.

Each of these types of sleep problems is understandable if you take into consideration your stages of sleep.

Table 3: A description of the stages of sleep.

Stages of sleep	
Stage 1	This is a transitional stage from wakefulness to sleep. It is associated with very light sleep. During this stage, muscle activity slows down.
Stage 2	During this stage, your sleep starts to deepen. Your breathing pattern changes and slows as does your heart rate. Your body temperature drops slightly.
Stage 3	It is at this stage that deep sleep begins to be experienced. To signal the onset of deep sleep, your brain starts to generate slow delta waves.
Stage 4	This is when you are most deeply asleep. During this stage, your muscle activity is limited.
REM sleep	This refers to Rapid Eye Movement Sleep. It occurs when you are at the closest point to wakefulness. It is associated with vivid dreaming. During this stage, your heart rate increases.

Over the course of the night, you will cycle through these stages. For the first half or so of the night, you will cycle down into the deep sleep associated with stages 3 and 4. However, as the night progresses, the cycling pattern is lighter and does not involve deep sleep. This pattern is demonstrated in the diagram below. Periods of REM sleep occur at the point in the cycle when you are closest to waking.

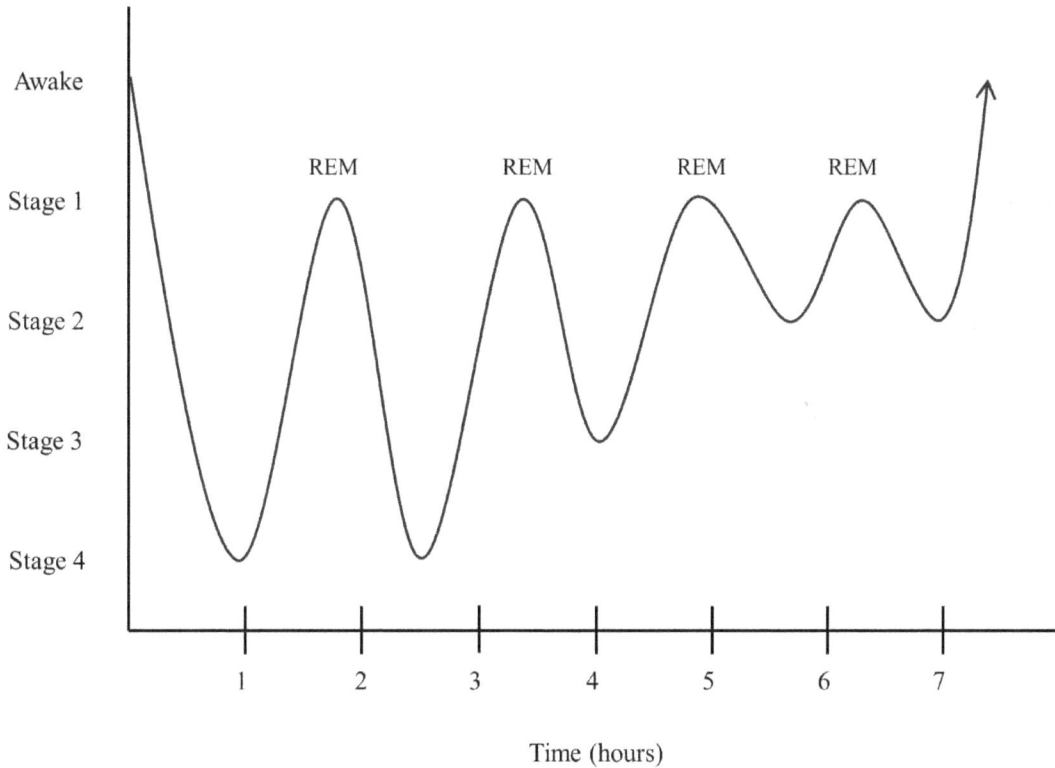

Figure 6: The cycles of sleep over the course of a sleep period.

When you have trouble falling asleep at the beginning of the night, you are struggling to enter into Stage 1 of sleep. This transitional stage is designed to pull you down into deeper sleep. Stage 1 allows you to do what your brain is inviting you to do, that is, go to sleep. Unfortunately, if you are stressed and worried, your nervous system is generally too aroused to allow this to occur. Your nervous system fights against this natural urge to sleep. Your worry thoughts are indicating to your brain that it is a good idea to stay awake in case something happens that you need to respond to.

When you have trouble staying asleep, you tend to wake up when your sleep cycle reaches those points where it is closest to wakefulness. In general, your nervous system is too aroused to allow you to stay asleep. Then, as soon as you wake, your mind turns to worry thoughts that then keep you awake until you can get back to sleep. This can happen numerous times throughout the night.

When you are troubled by waking early and being unable to return to sleep, this usually occurs in the second part of the night when you have moved past the deep sleep cycles. Your sleep is lighter, and when your nervous system is too aroused and you come close to wakefulness, you become completely awake, your worried thoughts begin, and you cannot get back to sleep.

What can I do about my sleep problems?

Each of these types of sleep disturbance can be influenced by racing thoughts. These thoughts are usually of a stressful nature. They increase your nervous system arousal, making it difficult to get any rest.

Here is a series of simple steps that should help you have a better night's sleep.

	Simple sleep strategy
1.	In the evening, avoid caffeine and sugary drinks and food.
2.	In the lead up to your bedtime, start to wind down. Turn off stimulating television or stop engaging in other activities around the house that cause you to feel more alert.
3.	Have a small snack rich in carbohydrates.
4.	Get into a comfortable bed and into a comfortable position. Slow your breathing. Relax your muscle tension.
5.	Give your mind something to think about that is not emotionally arousing. This could be writing a simple story in your head, listing in your mind all the countries you can think of, starting with A, then B, etc. Count backwards by 7s from a randomly selected number.
6.	If your thoughts drift to more stressful thoughts, acknowledge what is happening and then return to the activity you chose to keep your mind focused.
7.	Allow yourself to drift off to sleep.

Exercise available at elemen.com.au

The goal here is to create the right sort of internal environment to facilitate a good night's sleep. Avoid caffeine and sugary food or drinks because they can have a stimulating effect on your nervous system. In general, you should be aiming to 'turn off' by reducing the number of external stimulating activities. You do these things in preparation for sleep.

Carbohydrates can also increase your readiness for sleep. This is because carbohydrates contribute to an increase in your brain of a protein called tryptophan. This is a building block for a neurotransmitter called serotonin and a hormone called melatonin. Serotonin has a role in controlling sleep, appetite and mood. Melatonin release is triggered by darkness, and this hormone helps promote a regular sleep-wake cycle. This process, triggered by eating a carbohydrate-rich snack before bedtime, helps you sleep.

When your mind is already overrun by thoughts that are keeping you awake, it seems counterintuitive to give your brain something else to think about. However, it is not the thoughts themselves that will keep you awake. It is the nature of the thoughts that will have an effect on your sleep. In this way, you want to distract yourself from thinking stress-related thoughts, replacing them with thoughts that will not cause you to react emotionally. You should aim to keep your brain busy with mundane thoughts so that your mind is distracted from the stress-inducing thoughts. We like to refer to this activity as 'busy work' for your brain. It is the modern-day equivalent of counting sheep.

Mundane thoughts will allow you to drift off to sleep whereas stress-related thoughts will keep you alert and awake. Your brain is always active so it is not possible to stop thinking altogether. When you think of things that cause your nervous system to respond by increasing your arousal, you will have trouble sleeping. If you think calming or even boring thoughts, you brain will trigger the processes that lead you to falling asleep.

The same strategy of giving your mind something other than stressful things to think about can be applied if you awaken during the night. Simply get settled and focus on the mundane thoughts you have selected, allowing yourself to drift off back to sleep.

A worry decision tree

Here, we are going to learn how to choose to do something other than worry. This is not to say you are just going to tell yourself to stop worrying because that does not work. We are going to introduce a decision-making process that will help you replace your worried thoughts with more effective and appropriate thoughts for that moment. Consider the decision tree below.

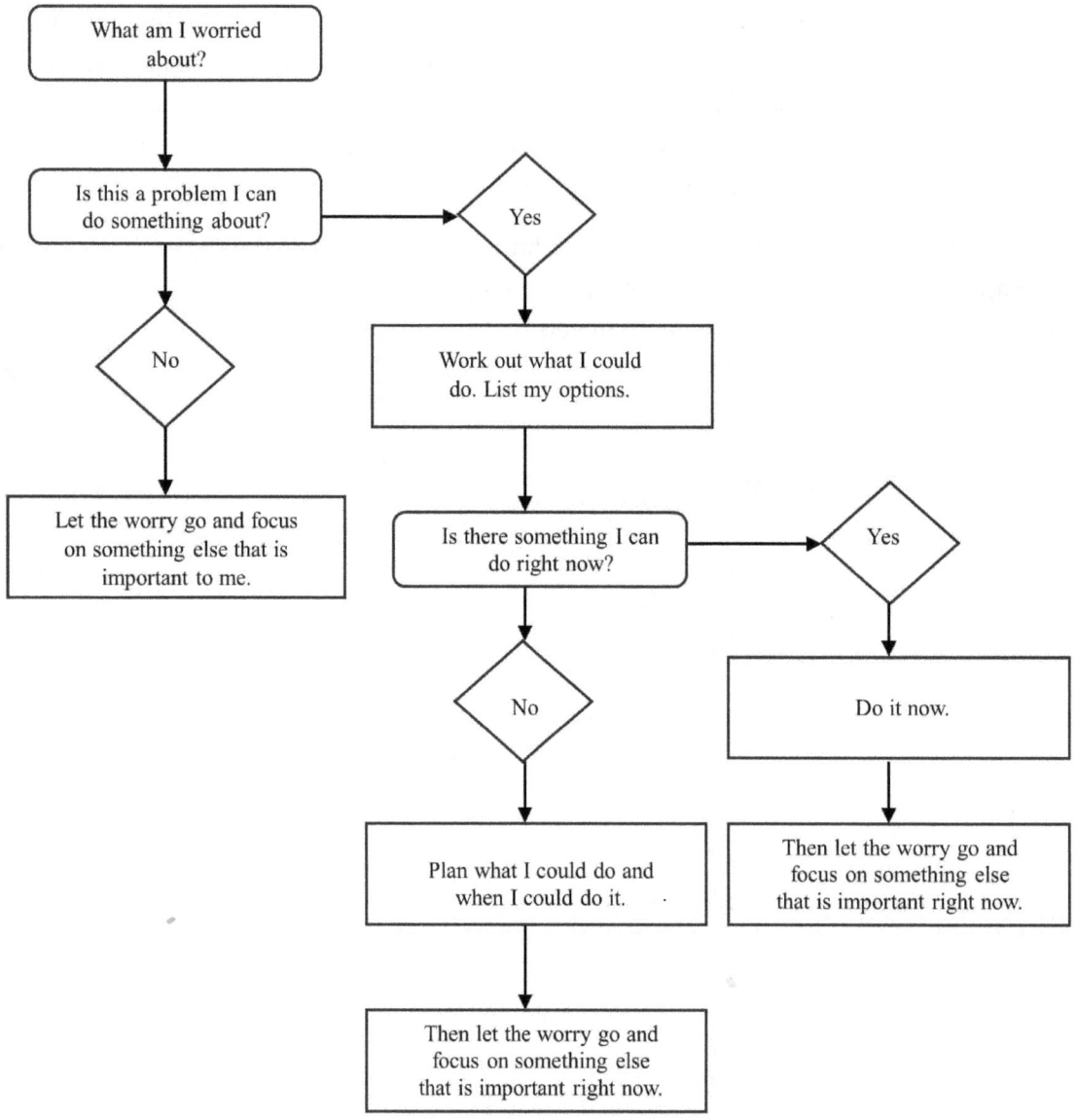

Figure 7: A worry decision tree.

When you catch yourself worrying, ask yourself what it is you are worrying about. Be as specific as possible. Too often when we are asked what it is we are worrying about, we will say things like "everything" or "I don't know". Here we are asking you to consider your worry thoughts to identify what it is that you are worrying about.

Then, ask yourself whether the thing you are worrying about is something you can do anything about. Very often, we worry about things that are not in our control. If you cannot think of any way you could control the thing you are worrying about, then let the worry go and deliberately replace those worry thoughts with something else to think about. You will get better at doing this with practice, but in the meantime, go looking for something that will distract you.

If you believe the thing you are worrying about is something you can control in some way, focus your attention on making a list of things you could do. Deliberate problem-solving is a better alternative to worrying. Remember, worriers are as good as non-worriers at solving their problems. So, when you are worrying about a specific problem, make a list of things that might be good solutions to the problem you are facing.

Then ask yourself whether there is anything you need to do right now. This is important. Remember that worry is future based. We want you to focus on the here and now.

If there is not anything you need to do right now, plan what you will do down the track when it is necessary to do so and identify when you will do it. Make a list if necessary, so that you will be ready when the time comes.

Once you have done this, let go of the worry and focus your thinking on something else that will distract you. There is no point going over in your mind things you have planned to do when it is not yet time to do those things.

If there is something you can do right now, then just go ahead and do it. What are you waiting for? The only way you will know if your plan is going to be effective is to try it out.

Once you have done it and there is nothing more for you to do for the time being, then let go of the worry and replace it with some other distracting thought. There is nothing more for you to do so you might as well think of something else.

If your worry thoughts creep back into your mind, and they will when you first start to tackle your worry thoughts, then just remind yourself you have done all that is necessary right at this moment and go back to doing and thinking something else.

Worry, emotion and behaviour

From the decision-tree exercise, it seems that it is ok for you to think about your problems as long as you are effectively problem-solving. It is not ok to continuously worry in an unproductive way about problems you might face in the future. All that does is take the pleasure out of the present.

One other thing we have to consider when looking at ways to manage your worry is the link between emotion and behaviour. Our emotional state drives us to behave in particular ways. For example, if you feel anxious, you might choose to stay at home and not go out into the community.

What we need to consider here is the link between worry, emotional state and behaviour. Understanding that there is good and productive, and bad and unproductive worry thoughts, we need to examine what would happen if you managed your worry. How would this affect your emotional state and, as a result, the choices you made for what you wanted to do? Let's consider an example.

Example of using the worry-emotion-behaviour link
What are you worrying about? *I am worrying about what I would do if I lost my job. There hasn't been any talk about me losing my job but they are making some changes in another department at work and I am worried they might make changes to my area and they might make my position redundant. There is no talk of them making any position redundant in the other department, but you never know.*
How is that making you feel? *This is making me feel really anxious. I am anxious about what would happen if I lost my job.*
What do you do as a consequence? *I have been lying awake at night worrying about losing my job. I am finding it hard to concentrate at work because of my anxiety. I have felt so anxious that I have cancelled a couple of activities with friends that had been arranged.*

What could you think instead?
I could think about the facts that I have available to me. There have been no changes proposed to my department at work. The proposed changes to the other department are not related to anticipated redundancies. I realised that there was nothing immediately apparent that I needed to worry about and no indication there was anything anticipated that I needed to be concerned about.
How would that make you feel?
I would feel relieved. My anxiety would go away.
What would you do as a consequence?
I would just get on with things that are happening in the present. I would enjoy work and I would engage in some social activities with my friends.

Below is a worksheet you can use to examine your worry-emotion-behaviour link.

The worry-emotion-behaviour link worksheet
What are you worrying about?
How is that making you feel?
What do you do as a consequence?
What could you think instead?

How would that make you feel?
What would you do as a consequence?

Worksheet available at elemen.com.au

By understanding the link between worry, emotion and behaviour, you can make adjustments to the way you think. This results in changes to your emotional state and the choices you make with regard to how you act or what you do can be positively affected.

To change the way you think, we need to start by considering one particularly difficult aspect of worry. Here, we are referring to the intolerance of uncertainty, which is a fundamental component of worrying thoughts.

Managing uncertainty

One of the fundamental features of worry is an inability to tolerate uncertainty. This inability to tolerate uncertainty can justify worrying in your own mind. You think that because you cannot stand uncertainty, worrying will help make the future more predictable by preparing you for what might happen.

This process of worrying to reduce uncertainty creates a problem. Because worrying can be perceived as making life more predictable (although it does not actually do this), you just keep worrying to remove any uncertainty in your life. You end up worrying and worrying to manage something that is never resolved. That is, your inability to tolerate uncertainty remains unchanged.

Worrying may make you think you have control of the unpredictability of life but, in fact, life is as unpredictable and uncertain as it has always been. Indeed, this belief that you have control does not stop you from feeling anxious or stop you from worrying.

Challenging your uncertainty

The first step in addressing the problem of the inability to tolerate uncertainty is to learn to effectively challenge this intolerance. Let's challenge this intolerance by considering the following questions.

Can you be entirely certain about everything in life?

> In reality, the answer is no. No matter how much you strive for certainty, the fact of the matter is that it cannot be achieved in all things. This is because the future is unknown as it has not yet happened.

Are there any advantages to needing certainty?

> Here, we are not talking about <u>having</u> certainty because we have already determined it is not possible to be entirely certain about everything in life. So, how has <u>needing</u> certainty been advantageous. It is hard to think of a single advantage. It might seem like it makes you prepared for the future but, if that was the case, you would just stop worrying. But you do not. The only things that needing certainty creates are negative things.

What are the disadvantages of needing certainty?

> Here, we can generate a long list of negative consequences of needing certainty. For example, needing certainty causes you to worry. It causes you to feel anxious and on edge. It takes away pleasure you might experience in relation to things that are happening in the present. It blocks you from being focused on the present and on things you can control. It makes you feel frustrated and unhappy.

Is your uncertainty the thing that is causing you to anticipate bad things will happen in the future?

>Is your uncertainty causing you to anticipate all these bad things in the future? In all likelihood, yes. If you think about it, you could just as easily predict good things or neutral things happening in the future. There is no reason only to predict bad things… except for your feelings of uncertainty.

How good are you at predicting the future?

>Here, we are asking you to consider the likelihood that the things you predict will turn out that way. You do not have a special ability to accurately predict bad things. Why would your ability to predict good or neutral things not be just as strong as your ability to predict bad things? In fact, your ability to predict the future has nothing to do with your tendency to predict bad things. It is your current feeling of uncertainty that is causing the problem. If you can see that the likelihood of the outcome you predict happening is low, could you find a way to just live with that low level of risk?

Are there some uncertainties you can just accept?

>If you think about it, there are some uncertainties that you accept. These will be different for each of you. However, it is the case that even the more prolific worriers will accept a multitude of things despite a general tendency to be uncertain about the future. For example, you might not know when your sister will be in touch next, but you accept that she will contact you. You might not know the exact date of your next car service, but you assume you will just book the car for a service when you need to do so. You might not know what you will feel like eating for dinner throughout the week, but you will accept that you will cook something. If you give it some thought, there are probably many times when you disregard uncertainty without feeling anxious. Why not apply the same strategy you use to disregard the uncertainty and low level of risk you use for these things to the times when you are focused on uncertainty and are worried about the future?

Accepting uncertainty

So, how do you accept uncertainty? It is pretty straightforward. Remember, you are worrying because you are time travelling, that is, you are focused on future events and anticipating poor outcomes. What would happen if you could just let go of the focus on the future and spend more time focusing on the present? We have already covered some mindfulness activities that should help you quiet your mind by focusing on what is happening in the here and now.

Here, we are asking you to do three things.

Catch yourself worrying

> Notice when you are thinking worrying thoughts. Acknowledge that you are worrying because you feel uncertain about the future. To start, all you have to do is acknowledge that these thoughts are present.

Let go of your worrying thoughts

> Do not give your worrying thoughts more attention than they need. Do not go over them in your mind. Also, do not start a battle with your thoughts, trying to force them away. Just let them drift away. You might be able to achieve this by imagining your thoughts floating on a leaf down a river or floating away like the clouds. Remind yourself that they are only thoughts, and you can decide whether you have them in your mind. Remind yourself that not knowing exactly what will happen in the future is the same for everyone, and you will just deal with things if they arise.

Avoid self-criticism and judgments

> Especially early on in this process of practising how to think differently, you may find that your thoughts drift back to the worrying ones. Accept this as normal and not as a sign that you have failed. These thoughts have just come back into your mind and now you will allow them to drift away again. Encourage yourself to stay focused on the present by allowing your attention to go to what is happening around you <u>right now</u>.

By learning to control your need for certainty, you are changing the way you are thinking. You are choosing to think in a helpful way rather than in an anxious and worrying way. There are other ways to address your thinking, including your tendency to catastrophise about the future.

Changing your worry thinking

In this workbook, we have indicated that the way we think about the things we experience influences how we react to them. We have touched on this when we considered learning about the worry-emotion-behaviour link. To feel better, we might have to change the way we view something so that we are not vulnerable to distressed reactions to events that we cannot control and cannot predict with certainty. Let's think of ways we can challenge unhelpful thinking and replace it with the types of thoughts that allow us to see things more clearly and choose behaviours that will help us.

How are our thoughts affected?

As we go through life, we can develop unhelpful thinking styles or errors in our thinking. These errors influence how we interpret the world around us and how we fit into that world. In an attempt to make sense of the world, we develop 'templates' or models of how we think things should work.

For example, you might develop a template that tells you that to be a worthwhile person, everyone should like you. On the surface, this seems workable. It is nice when people like you and it makes you feel good, including feeling good about yourself. However, if you have a template that you are worthwhile only if everyone likes you, what happens if, for some reason, someone chooses not to like you? You then become upset about something that really is an ordinary enough experience. You then feel like you are not worthwhile, even in situations where the fact that the other person does not like you says more about them than it does about you. We have found that people choose not to like others for the oddest of reasons. For example, one person disclosed that they found they could not like people who even vaguely looked like a cousin they did not admire. Should your feelings of self-worth be affected by the fact that you look somewhat like a person you have never met? It is obvious that the answer is no. Unfortunately, your template might tell you that to be a worthwhile person, *everyone* has to like you. You can see the problem.

Our individual templates are put together based on information from a variety of sources, including, for example, our personality and our experiences throughout life. If the messages we receive from our experiences in life are good and healthy ones, we tend to have good and healthy templates of how the world works and how we fit into that world. However, if the messages are distorted in some way (e.g., being told you have to be the best at everything you do, that no one will like you if you disagree with them, your needs are not as important as other people's needs, that bad things will happen if you are not paying attention), then the templates we develop will reflect these messages and will be unhelpful.

Core beliefs

So, how do these templates affect us? They tells us how we should respond when dealing with our world and the people in it. The information we gather determines our 'core beliefs' about three things:

> How safe or dangerous we perceive the world to be.
> Our place in that world and our value as a person.
> How certain the future feels.

These core beliefs are not the 'truth' of things. They develop as a result of the information we gather along the way in life, whether or not that information is helpful or unhelpful, clear or confusing, or accurate or distorted.

If we have helpful, clear and accurate templates, then our core beliefs are healthy, and our thinking does not contain errors about how the world works, how we fit into that world and how safe the future might be. However, if we have unhelpful, confusing and distorted templates, our thinking contains errors that affect how we react to the world and how we view ourselves in that world.

Cognitive errors

Cognitive errors are the errors in thinking that occur when our templates of how the world works and how we fit into that world send us the wrong message. Our thinking about our experiences is then altered by the wrong message. Problems arise when we engage in certain types of cognitive errors.

Below are some of the most common cognitive errors. As you read through them, think about whether these types of errors occur in your thinking.

Table 4: Descriptions of the common errors in thinking.

Types of errors in thinking	
Error type	*Error in thinking*
Filtering	A person whose thinking is affected by filtering takes the negative details of an event and exaggerates them while filtering out any positive aspects of the situation. For example, a person who worries all the time will focus on one time that things did not work out so well for them and ignore all the other times that things worked out just fine.

Polarised thinking	With polarised thinking, things are either 'black or white' or 'all or nothing'. People who think this way place situations in 'either/or' categories, with no middle ground to account for the complexity of most situations. For example, a person who worries might believe that either the thing they are concerned about will not happen or it will happen and be a complete disaster. They cannot see that something might happen, but it turns out to be manageable or has little consequence.
Overgeneralisation	A person makes a conclusion based on one event or a single piece of information. In this way, if something bad happens to them on one occasion they expect it to happen over and over again. For example, a person who worries may believe that just because one bad thing happened on one occasion then all things will turn out the same even when there are different influences on the event.
Jumping to conclusions	If a person jumps to conclusions, they 'know' what the other person is thinking about without that person saying so. For example, a person who worries about how others think of them may be convinced that a person views them as hopeless despite that person never saying so or indicating that this is the view they hold.
Catastrophising	A person who catastrophises expects disaster to strike, no matter what. A person hears about a problem and uses *what-if* questions to imagine the worst outcome. For example, a person who worries will believe that the likely outcome of anything that concerns them will be the most negative and the most extreme outcome.
Personalisation	A person believes that everything others do or say is some kind of direct, personal reaction to them. They take everything personally. For example, a person who worries might misinterpret another person's preoccupation as an indication of their withdrawal from them.
Control fallacies	This occurs when a person strongly endorses the view that all things are controlled and controllable. This can occur in two ways. Firstly, there is external control where the person feels they are a helpless victim of fate or, secondly, internal control where a person assumes responsibility for the pain and unhappiness of others. For example, a person who worries may believe that nothing they do can make any difference because the world is conspiring against them.

Fallacy of fairness	A person who believes they know what is fair will feel resentful and unhappy if others disagree with them. People who judge every event in their lives in terms of whether or not it is fair will often feel resentful, angry and hopeless. For example, a person who worries may think it is unfair that they have to suffer in this way when other people do not have to suffer.
Blaming	This person holds other people responsible for their own emotional pain. Alternatively, they may blame themselves for every problem – even those clearly outside their control. For example, a person who worries may be self-critical and blame themselves for not changing their behaviour, even when they have not learned the strategies they need to be able to control their worry.
Shoulds	Should statements (e.g., I should visit my parents more) are made by people who hold rigid rules about how the world should work and how everyone should behave. Breaking these rules makes a person angry. They also feel guilty when they violate their own rules. For example, a person who worries may believe they absolutely should be prepared for every eventuality and worrying allows them to have this preparation.
Emotional reasoning	People with this distortion in thinking are guided by what they 'feel' is the truth. They will rely on their feelings to establish whether or not something is 'fact'. If a person feels stupid and boring, then they must be stupid and boring. Emotional reasoning blocks rationality and logic. For example, a person who worries believes that because they are worried, something terrible must happen without there being any evidence that this is so.
Fallacy of change	A person with this type of thinking believes that if they apply enough pressure, others will change to meet their needs. This person needs others to change because they cannot cope if others disagree with them or behave in ways that are contrary to how this person feels they should behave. For example, a person who worries may hold the view that others must heed their warnings that bad things could happen. When they dismiss these warnings, the worrier may nag and pressure the other person to get them to do as they demand.

Global labelling	A person generalises a small number of features or characteristics of themselves or others and inflates them into a global statement of judgment. This goes beyond overgeneralising. Rather than take into account the context of a situation, the person will apply this judgment to all aspects of a person or situation. For example, a person who worries may label themselves as unlucky in life, not because of what happens to them but because of the things they fear will happen.
Always being right	When a person engages in this error of thinking, they insist that all views held by them or actions done by them are correct. In their view, they cannot make a mistake or be misinformed. For example, a person who worries may believe they are correct in predicting dire outcomes and may do nothing to avoid bad things happening just to prove to others that they are right.
Heaven's reward fallacy	A person who engages in this type of thinking believes that a person's hard work and sacrifice will pay off in the end, as if someone is keeping track of what everyone does in life. Sharing some similarities with the fallacy of fairness thinking, this person believes that the one who does the most, works the hardest or sacrifices the most will be the person who is rewarded at some point in the future. For example, a person who worries may believe that they should not suffer in the way they do because they are good people who always do the right thing and try to help people.

Let's consider how these errors in thinking affect a person's point of view. Below are examples of these types of logical errors in thinking, along with a more rational point of view.

Table 5: Examples of rational and irrational perspectives for each error in thinking.

Correcting your thinking	
Error in thinking	*A rational view*
Filtering	
Joel went to the supermarket to do some grocery shopping. While he was there, someone parked in the bay beside him, must have opened their car door and hit his car, leaving a scrape mark on his car paintwork. Despite regularly parking in the supermarket carpark without incident, Joel then developed an overwhelming concern about potential damage to his car if he parked there again. He was so worried about this happening that he went out of his way to go to the supermarket late at night when it was not so busy and parked far away from other parked cars.	Rather than see what happened as an unusual event that had never happened before despite the large number of times he had parked in the supermarket carpark, Joel filtered out that information and focused only on the fact that on one occasion, his car had been mildly damaged. He then predicted this happening time and time again. Joel would have been better off considering all the information about parking in the supermarket carpark that he had available to him and reaching the conclusion that the risk was actually quite small that his car would be damaged every time he parked there.
Polarised thinking	
Stuart was worried about visiting the dentist. He had been putting off seeking dental care because he worried that it was going to be an unpleasant experience. He believed that he had two options. That is, either he had to avoid dental care, or he would have a terrible dental experience. Despite needing dental care, Stuart felt he could not expose himself to a terrible dental experience, so he opted to avoid the care he needed.	Stuart make the mistake of assuming that his experience was either one thing or another. He could not see that there were other alternative outcomes. He would have been better off considering that it was possible for more positive outcomes if he went ahead with a dental appointment. Believing that it was bound to be terrible, Stuart did not bother exploring his options for a more pleasant experience by talking with the staff at the dental practice.

Overgeneralisation	
Sophie was in a relationship with Mark. Mark was stressed because of work and was more irritable than usual. Mark snapped at Sophie because of a minor thing she did that annoyed him. Sophie became upset and Mark became frustrated and an argument developed. Sophie worried that her relationship with Mark was never going to work because they had failed to communicate well on this one occasion. Sophie ended the relationship with Mark, seeing no point in trying to work things out.	Sophie would have been better off to consider that one minor incident in the context of her other experiences with her boyfriend. Rather than this one argument reflecting an overall pattern of dysfunction in the relationship, it probably demonstrated nothing more than the fact that people become more irritable if they have had a bad day.
Jumping to conclusions	
Rebecca worried about everything. She had been a worrier for as long as she could remember. Rebecca's parents sat her down and talked to her about the idea of her getting some help with this problem. They said they had been concerned about what all this worry was doing to her happiness. They expressed genuine concern. Rebecca formed the view that her parents thought she was a hopeless mess who could never do anything right.	Rather than appreciating that their advice was a genuine expression of concern for her wellbeing, Rebecca jumped to the conclusion that her parents held her in very low regard. She would have been better off taking their advice at face value and not fabricating a story in her head about what she thought they 'really' meant.

Catastrophising	
Patricia forgot her friend's birthday. Usually, she sends a card and flowers to her friend, but this year, she simply forgot. Patricia worried that her friend would never forgive her and would never speak to her again, despite the fact that they had been friends for many years and her friend was a very understanding person.	Patricia formed a view about what would happen as a consequence of her failure to remember her friend's birthday that was completely inconsistent with what she knew about her friend. Given that their friendship had endured for many years and given that her friend was known to be understanding, the chances that her friend would be so hurt by Patricia's mistake that their friendship would fail were very slim. Patricia was reacting to her own emotional response to her failing to remember her friend's birthday rather than predicting a likely future. In any case, Patricia would not know how her friend had responded until she spoke with her friend about the matter. Predicting a terrible future does not increase the chances that a terrible future will happen, especially if the prediction is based on incorrect information.

Personalisation	
Julia's best friend had not been in touch for a couple of weeks. Julia was aware that her friend's mother had been very ill and in hospital. Julia lay awake at night worrying about what she had done to offend her friend.	In reality, it seems that Julia's best friend had a lot on her plate to deal with. It is unlikely, then, that the cause of her failure to be in touch was an indiscretion on Julia's part that even Julia could not identify. Sometimes, the simplest explanation is the best one. Julia's friend was busy caring for her mother, and her failure to keep in touch had nothing to do with Julia.

Control fallacies	
Andrea was told that if she did not start getting her assignments in on time, she would fail the course she was undertaking. Andrea had been putting off doing the work she needed to do, worrying that she would find the task too difficult, before she had even tried. Despite the warning, Andrea still did not do anything to start the work she needed to do to submit her outstanding assignments. She believed that there was nothing she could do to make things better and that there was no point in trying because nothing ever worked out for her. She was right to worry, she believed, because the world was conspiring against her to prevent her from achieving her ambitions in life.	By believing that there was a force external to her that was determining how her life played out, Andrea never did anything to change the course of her life or influence the outcome of the challenges she faced. By changing her thinking about the controls she thinks are influencing her life, Andrea could open herself up to the idea that she can make positive choices for herself that would contribute to good outcomes.

Fallacies of fairness	
Jacqueline was very unhappy with her sisters. She felt that they got along well with each other, and she was the outsider. At one family occasion, she confronted her sisters who were laughing about things that had happened to them. She told them it was not fair that they could look at life so lightly and not be burdened by the worry she had to endure. Jacqueline said that if her sister's could not appreciate her difficulties then she wanted nothing to do with them. Jacqueline's sisters were shocked by her claims and her reaction to them enjoying the family get-together. They knew they had a more optimistic view of life than did Jacqueline but they did not know she was so resentful about it	Jacqueline thought it was unfair that her sisters had an easier passage through life because of their easier outlook on life and sunnier worldview. Jacqueline should have considered that she could have a less pessimistic view if she had learned to challenge her thinking and replace it with more realistic thinking. Although Jacqueline had been thinking otherwise, the truth is that the world is neither fair nor unfair; it is just the way it is. By altering her thinking, Jacqueline may be more inclined to see that she was not a victim of an unfair world. Instead, she had got herself into a difficult situation by endlessly worrying about things that might happen… but probably would not happen.

Blaming

Jasper knew his worrying was making him unhappy and was causing his wife to feel exasperated. Jasper had just spent an uncomfortable weekend, feeling miserable about what he might be facing at work in the coming week. His boss announced that he was changing some team structures and dividing the work differently so that there would be a more even distribution between teams in terms of workload and responsibilities. Even though his boss had recently highlighted that Jasper was on a team that was overburdened with work, so he was likely to have his workload lightened, he worried all weekend about whether he would be given more to do.

Jasper's wife got fed up with his worrying about this matter. Indeed, she was so exasperated by it that she took the children and went out for the day without him. Intellectually, Jasper could see that there was probably nothing to worry about, but he just could not let the worry go. He also knew he was driving his wife crazy. Jasper blamed himself for making things so difficult. He knew he had to stop doing this and was self-critical for failing to change when he knew that he should

The bottom line is that Jasper was making things worse by blaming himself for still worrying when he realised he should do otherwise. Jasper did not acknowledge that if he could have done otherwise, he would have done so. But Jasper did not know how to stop worrying. He could not know what he did not know. If Jasper could realise that by learning some strategies to help him stop worrying, he could change the way he approached things and stop blaming himself for things that, at the moment, he cannot control.

Shoulds	
Craig was worried about his future and the future of his family. He worried that they would not be financially secure. Craig sought the advice of a financial advisor who reassured him that he was in a good position for this stage in life and that, if he kept on track, things would be fine. But Craig worried that he should be doing more. He felt he should be saving more. Despite the advice he received, he believed he should work harder and make better investments. He felt he had an obligation to do this. He felt he should get a second job… just in case. Craig's wife did not want him to do that. She believed that Craig would be happier if he could focus on enjoying his life and he should choose to spend more time with his family.	Craig was being driven by the rigid rules he set for himself about preparedness for the future. He ignored the advice he received and his wife's wishes in favour of his driven pursuit of a more secure future. Craig would have been better off realising that a better quality of life could be achieved by a more balanced approach to how he managed his life. Without any flexibility in the rules he set for himself, he was depriving himself of pleasure in life

Emotional reasoning	
Suzanne was convinced her husband was going to leave her despite his reassurances to the contrary. Suzanne felt she had no redeeming qualities and believed she was unlovable. In her mind, Suzanne believed that her husband could not love her because she was unlovable and he would realise this and leave. Suzanne was worrying endlessly. She felt that there was a high likelihood that her husband would leave. After all, why would she feel so anxious if there was not something to worry about.	Suzanne has this the wrong way around. She has a strong emotional reaction that is based on her views about herself, and because of this strong emotional reaction, she concludes that her view that her husband could not love her is true. She believes this strongly despite the lack of objective evidence. Rather than holding the view that because she is upset, what she fears must be true, Suzanne should identify an existing problem based on objective evidence and then decide how much emotional energy she is going to give to the problem. So, problem first, emotional response second, not emotional response first, and generate a problem second.

Fallacy of change	
Although they were only in their 60s, Andrew was worried about his parents' situation. Despite them being happy, active, and healthy and living in the home they owned, Andrew felt it was necessary that they urgently consider their future. He told them they needed to start looking at a retirement home because he worried about what would happen when they could no longer manage their home. He told them they needed to start getting serious about life and accept that they were getting older. Andrew's parents dismissed his concerns. They considered they were well set up for the future. But Andrew would not accept that was the case. He continually nagged them, determined that he would get them to do what he thought they should do. Andrew knew that he would feel terrible if his parents' situation in the future was not secure because they had not listened to his warnings.	Andrew made the mistake of assuming that the things that were concerning for him were going to be concerning for his parents. In fact, his parents were in a better position to know of their own circumstances. Nevertheless, Andrew believed that if he pressured them enough, they would do as he said. However, all Andrew was doing was driving a wedge between him and his parents and damaging their relationship. He would have been better off if he had realised that, as adults, his parents could make their own choices, even if they were not the ones Andrew thought they should make.
Global labelling	
Brad was convinced he was unlucky in life and that nothing would ever work out in his favour. He thought that lucky people did not have to worry about all the things that concerned him about the dire future he predicted. Although he was lonely, Brad decided not to pursue a relationship with a person who expressed their interest in him. After all, because he was unlucky, he believed the relationship would never work. Although he liked this person very much, his unluckiness in life made it pointless to consider a relationship.	In truth, there is no such thing as luck. Good things do happen to people, as do bad things, but not because of some inherent characteristic known as luckiness that determines the outcome in people's lives. It would have helped Brad to realise that he was missing out on life because of this distorted view of how the world works. He labelled himself as unlucky, so he saw no point in wanting things that other people have. If he was able to remove that label and see that although sometimes bad things happen, so do good things, then he would be able to leave himself open to opportunities in life that might come his way.

Always being right	
Isla's family knew she was a worrier. Although they sometimes teased her about it, they would also become annoyed with her when she would not do anything to help herself, seemingly to prove that she was right in her dire predictions about the future. Isla was being bullied at work. Isla's family listened to her concerns and gave her advice about the avenues open to her to do something about it. But Isla simply refused to do anything to stand up for herself or seek assistance from her employer. Isla had repeatedly told them that bad things were likely to happen to her but her family had just dismissed her worries. Isla thought that they would now see that she had been right.	In an effort to prove herself right, Isla refused to do anything to change her situation and help herself. From Isla's perspective she thought it was better to prove that she was justified in being worried than acting to change her life circumstances. Isla could have attempted to solve her problems if only she could see that her need to be right was interfering with her taking charge of aspects of her life. Proving herself right was providing her with no real advantage.

Heaven's reward fallacy	
Chloe always put other people's needs before her own. She ran around after people, listened to their problems, and looked after their children and pets. However, when Chloe was worried about things in her life, she was surprised by the response of her friends to her requests for help. She found they did not really take the time to listen to her problems and help her despite all of the effort she had put into caring for them. Chloe's feelings were hurt, and she was confused by her friends' failure to meet her needs at times when she really needed their help.	Chloe made the mistake of believing that because she had done the right thing, other people would do the same. Everyone is driven by their own motivations. Each person sets the standard for their own behaviour. Although it would be nice if people reciprocated, there is simply no guarantee that will happen when you enter into a relationship with another person.

It is apparent that these types of logical errors do not make things easy for us. Quite the opposite. They lead us to misinterpret events so that we adopt a limited or negative perspective that colours how we view things, our emotional responses, and the choices of how we behave as a consequence.

Why do we think in unhelpful ways?

Why do we think in ways that are distorted and not particularly helpful? To understand why errors in thinking happen, we have to consider the theory behind cognitive behaviour therapy (CBT). According to this theory, our thinking has more than one level. This is displayed in the diagram below.

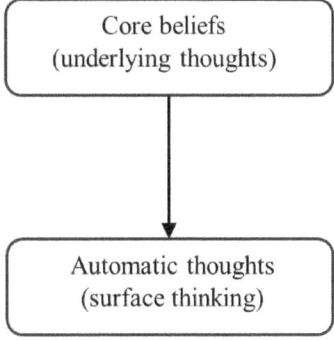

Figure 8: A diagram of the two levels of thought.

Automatic thoughts refer to the running commentary that goes through our minds as we go about our daily lives. If you pay attention, you will notice the constant chatter that goes on in your head about the things you are doing and how you are reacting to the people and events around you.

There is an easy exercise that will show you how this running commentary works. For the next minute, think about a bowl of fruit. Over the course of the minute, just let your thoughts do what they want as you think about a bowl of fruit. At the end of the minute, notice where your thoughts have taken you. Now consider the links between your starting point (thinking about a bowl of fruit) and where you ended up (thinking whatever it was you were thinking). Consider below how this might have played out for one individual. This person started thinking about a bowl of fruit and ended up thinking about how badly they needed a haircut. Follow their automatic thoughts.

> *Ok. I'm thinking about a bowl of fruit. I can picture a bowl of fruit. It's got bananas in it. I like bananas. I should buy some next time I go to the supermarket. I also need to get a loaf of bread. I must start a shopping list. Pay attention and think about a bowl of fruit. Oh, and milk, I mustn't forget milk. I hate running out of milk. Someone said once that they have orange juice on their cereal instead of milk. Yuck. I couldn't imagine anything worse. Not that I eat much cereal. I should eat more cereal… it's probably good for you. I will put cereal on my shopping list. But that might be a waste because I probably won't eat it. I have bought lots of things I thought would be good for me, but I never ate them. That reminds me that I should clean out the pantry. I never have time to clean out the pantry. I have so much to do. I can't even find time to make an appointment with the hairdresser. I really need a haircut.*

At the other level of thinking, we have what is known as core beliefs. Core beliefs refer to the underlying beliefs we have about how the world works and how we fit into that world. Core beliefs have influence on our automatic thoughts. That is, we think the things we do on the surface because of our underlying beliefs about how things work. Unlike automatic thoughts, the content of our core beliefs is not readily available to us but can be examined by considering the content of our automatic thoughts.

So, where do the logical errors in thinking we have been talking about fit into this conceptualisation? Let's consider that in the diagram below.

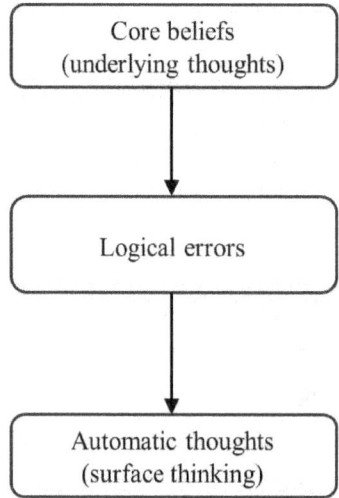

Figure 9: Where errors in thinking occur in our levels of thought.

The errors in thinking we make are a result of the core beliefs we hold. For example, if our core beliefs about the world and the future are that the world is threatening and the outlook is grim and pessimistic, then we are likely to inflate the degree of dangerousness we perceive and we are likely to catastrophise.

These logical errors then affect our surface thinking. For example, we are more likely to tell ourselves everything is hopeless or tell ourselves that only bad things will happen because of the logical errors we make based on our particular core beliefs.

Our core beliefs are built on the basis of a variety of influences. These include our genetic makeup (e.g., an inherited overly reactive nervous system), our experiences (the things that happen to us), the messages we receive (the things people have said to us or the way they have treated us), and the ways we have interpreted these events. If the influences are positive and healthy, our core beliefs tend to be clear, and there are few logical errors. If the influences on us are negative, unhealthy or confusing, our core beliefs tend to be inaccurate, and the logical errors we make are many and strongly influence our automatic thoughts.

Underlying assumptions of logical errors

It has been suggested that each logical error is driven by specific assumptions. If our automatic thoughts are biased, then the biases are driven by our core beliefs and assumptions. Below are some examples of cognitive errors and examples of associated assumptions. Here we are referring to the assumptions that are inevitably made if the errors in our thinking are present.

Table 6: The assumptions underlying each logical error.

Cognitive error	Assumption
Filtering	The only events that matter are failures. I should measure myself by my errors.
Polarised thinking	Everything is always one extreme or the other.
Overgeneralisation	If it's true in one case, it must be true in every case that is even slightly similar.
Jumping to conclusions	If it has always been true in the past, it is going to be true in the future.
Catastrophising	Always think the worst because it is most likely to happen to you.
Personalisation	I am responsible for all bad things, failures, etc.
Control fallacies	You should be able to know in advance what is going to happen. You should have seen the bad thing coming before it happened.

Fallacy of fairness	The world is a fair place, and fairness will influence how things turn out.
Blaming	Whether it is me or someone else, someone is always responsible when things are not the way I want them to be.
Shoulds	People have an obligation to do specific things that cannot be avoided.
Emotional reasoning	If a person feels bad, something must be wrong.
Fallacy of change	People must change to meet other people's needs.
Global labelling	A whole person and their entire life can be summed up by a single word (e.g., stupid).
Always being right	People have to choose a side, and there is a right side and a wrong side.
Heaven's reward fallacy	Choosing to do good things for others will oblige others to do good things in return.

Let's consider how these logical errors and assumptions affect automatic thoughts. Consider in this example what this person is saying to themselves about something they are worrying about. Let's go back to the person who is worried about losing their job because a different department in their organisation is being restructured.

> *I just know I'm going to lose my job. I just know it. They will get around to restructuring my department, and they will get rid of people, and I will be one of them* (catastrophising). *This sort of thing has happened before. There are lots of cases where restructuring has resulted in redundancies. This is bound to happen again* (jumping to conclusions). *In fact, this happened to a friend. She worked in a government agency, and they restructured her department, and she ended up accepting a redundancy. If it could happen to her... and it did... it will happen to me* (overgeneralisation).

Let's break this down and see where this person is making mistakes.

Firstly, without this person's department being considered for restructuring, this person has predicted that this will happen. Also, despite there being no evidence of redundancies in the department that is being restructured, this person has assumed that redundancies will happen when their department is restructured and that they will be one of the people who would be forced to take a redundancy. This person had outlined the worst case scenario. It is evidence of catastrophic thinking.

Secondly, in general terms, this person was able to identify that there had been cases of restructuring leading to redundancies in the past. Without there being any connection to their current situation, they had made the assumption that because it has happened before, it will happen again in their case. This is evidence of the logical error of jumping to conclusions.

Thirdly, they had identified a specific case of redundancy to justify their need to worry. Because they know of one case of redundancy associated with restructuring, they have assumed that this will happen in all cases of restructuring. This is evidence of overgeneralisation.

The errors in this person's thinking have resulted in them feeling much worse than they would have if they had not made these errors. Let's find out how to change this way of thinking to protect yourself from the negative effects of logical errors.

Understanding automatic thoughts

The goal here is to teach you to think in a more realistic and balanced way so that you can cope better with your need to worry. This is done in a number of steps. Let's start this process.

Everybody experiences automatic thoughts. They reflect our way of making sense of and reacting to the world around us and to internal experiences, such as anxiety or memories and urges. Automatic thoughts are often highly believable, even when they are based on logical errors. As a result of their believability, we tend not to challenge them. If they pass unchallenged, they can have a profound and detrimental effect on our emotional state. For example, if a person believes their job is at risk and they do not challenge that thought, they are likely to feel anxious and threatened.

Consider this example.

> *It looks like my job is on the line. They are restructuring that other department, so there is no reason why they would not do the same with our department. There hasn't been any word about redundancies, but that doesn't mean there won't be. And it would be just my luck that I would be one of the people who will lose their job.*

It would be hard to think this way without feeling bad as a consequence. We tend to believe the things we tell ourselves. Even when we do not pay much attention to our self-talk – our running commentary – we can still be affected by it.

Catching automatic thoughts

It is important to pay attention to your automatic thoughts so that their content can be used to identify both the logical errors you are making and, ultimately, your core beliefs. The way to start this is to keep a thought record related to times when you notice a change in the way you are feeling.

In their simplest form, a thought record asks you to identify the event that has occurred, to take notice of the thoughts that go through your head at the time of the event, and to record the consequences you experience, both in terms of how you feel and how you might act in response. Consider the example below of a simple thought record.

A	B	C
Activating event	Belief or thought	Consequence: emotional and behavioural
I overheard two colleagues at work talking about the changes being made in the other department that is being restructured.	*We're next. I am going to lose my job.*	*I felt really anxious. I struggled to concentrate at work. I felt so bad I told my supervisor I was sick and I went home.*
A friend from the other department told me they were told there would be no redundancies.	*I thought it was only a matter of time before they changed their minds. Restructures always lead to redundancies.*	*I felt quite anxious about the future. I started looking for another job.*

We do not usually pay much attention to the thoughts that go through our heads, even though they can have such a profound effect on how we are feeling and what we choose to do as a result of feeling that way. To change our thinking, we have to learn to identify our automatic thoughts. When we consider the events that trigger a response in us, we can usually identify what went through our mind at the time.

By keeping track of your automatic thoughts, you can learn of patterns in your thinking that are linked with particular negative feelings and the behaviours you choose because you are feeling that way. Use the simple thought record below to keep track of your automatic thoughts in relation to events that stress you.

Simple automatic thoughts worksheet		
A	B	C
Activating event	Belief or thought	Consequence: emotional and behavioural

Worksheet available in elemen.com.au

Understanding and noticing logical errors

Everyone makes logical errors. It is important to understand this point. It is when the error you are making (e.g., everything should be fair) conflicts with how things really are (e.g., the world is neither fair nor unfair; it just is the way it is) that problems arise. However, it is also important to be able to recognise the logical errors you are making so that you can correct them and correct the problems in your core beliefs. To do this, you can try the simple approach of expanding on your thought record form so that you include the types of logical errors that are reflected in your automatic thoughts.

Let's go back to our original thought record form and expand the examples.

Expanded thought record form - example			
A	B	C	D
Activating event	Belief or thought	Consequence: emotional and behavioural	Logical errors
I overheard two colleagues at work talking about the changes being made in the other department that is being restructured.	*We're next. I am going to lose my job.*	*I felt really anxious. I struggled to concentrate at work. I felt so bad I told my supervisor I was sick and I went home.*	*Catastrophising.*
A friend from the other department told me they were told there would be no redundancies.	*I thought it was only a matter of time before they changed their minds. Restructures always lead to redundancies.*	*I felt quite anxious about the future. I started looking for another job.*	*Jumping to conclusions.*

With the first activating event, this person predicted the worst-case scenario. From changes taking place in a different department, this person predicted that their department would also face a restructuring even though there was no evidence of that. Further, it was predicted that there would be redundancies, despite no evidence, and that they would be one of the people who would be made redundant. This is an example of catastrophising. They have blown the information they had available to them out of proportion, predicting the worst possible outcome they feared would happen.

With the second activating event, despite being told that the changes in the other department did not involve redundancies, the person believed that all restructuring involved redundancies. Therefore, this restructuring would also involve redundancies. Further, because they felt driven to look for another job, they assumed that the imagined restructuring of their own department would result in redundancies, and they would lose their job. This is an example of jumping to conclusions. Without evidence, and just because they believed that restructuring and redundancies always existed together, they reached the conclusion that redundancies would occur, and they started looking for another job.

Below is an expanded thought record form that you can use to identify the logical errors in what you are thinking.

Expanded thought record form			
A	B	C	D
Activating event	Belief or thought	Consequence: emotional and behavioural	Logical errors

Worksheet available at elemen.com.au

Reframing your thoughts (cognitive restructuring)

The process of challenging our negative automatic thoughts is called cognitive restructuring. This is what we are trying to achieve here. The conclusions we reach because of our logical errors should be challenged and replaced with something that is healthier and more accurately reflects how the world really works.

Although there are lots of ways you can go about restructuring your thinking, we are going to introduce you to a straightforward method. We are going to start by ensuring that you understand the difference between fact and opinion. This is important as our thoughts and decision-making should be based on facts and not the opinions we form because of incorrect information that can underlie our core beliefs. For example, an opinion would be "I am stupid". You might form this opinion because someone has repeatedly told you that you are stupid or because they acted in a way that encouraged you to believe you were stupid. It is not the truth or a fact that you are stupid, even if you have done some things that are unwise. It is a belief you have or an opinion you have formed because of incorrect information.

We refer to the opinion on which you rely as a work of fiction. That is, you write a story in your head about what is happening and then act as if the story is true. You need to be able to identify when you are relying on the story you have written in your mind rather than basing your thoughts on factual evidence. Let's start by having a go at identifying fact from opinion or fiction. In the spaces provided, you can add other things you have been thinking and consider whether they are facts or opinions.

Fact or fiction worksheet		
Statement	*Fact*	*Fiction*
I am stupid		√
I love bushwalking	√	
I am ugly		
I forgot to renew my driver's licence		
No one likes me		
This will be a disaster		
I'm not good enough		
I hate my job		

I should have known what was about to happen		
There are times when people feel stressed		

Checklist available at elemen.com.au

The facts here are:

    I love bushwalking

    I forgot to renew my driver's licence

    I hate my job

    There are times when people feel stressed

The statements that are opinions are:

    I am stupid

    I am ugly

    No one likes me

    This will be a disaster

    I'm not good enough

    I should have known what was about to happen

Why should we make this distinction between what is a fact and what is an opinion? It is because the errors in thinking we make are based on opinion and not on fact. Further, because we hold this opinion, we assume that it is true because we are thinking it and not because it is based on fact.

To tidy up our thinking and remove the logical errors, we have to rely on those thoughts that are based on fact alone. We can reject thoughts that are just based on our opinions because our opinions can be faulty. Factual information will be a good guide for us to determine whether or not we should believe what we are thinking.

Cognitive restructuring worksheet: Example
What I am thinking *I think that my department will be the next to be restructured, and I will be made redundant.*
Facts supporting the thought *I can't think of any actual facts.*
Facts contradicting the thought *The restructuring is not taking place in my department.* *There has been no mention of a restructuring in my department.* *The staff in the other department have been told there will be no redundancies.* *There has been no discussion of redundancies in my department.*
Is this thought based on factual evidence or opinion? *This thought that my department would be restructured and I would be made redundant is based on opinion only. I suppose I am thinking this way without any real evidence.*

By looking at the facts for and against a point of view being true, you can work out the value of holding that opinion. It seems like a waste of time to be thinking a particular thing and being negatively affected by it emotionally and behaviourally if you cannot even determine that the opinion reflects the truth. You can use the worksheet below to examine your thoughts in terms of the facts supporting what you are thinking and the facts that contradict what you are thinking.

Cognitive restructuring worksheet
What I am thinking
Facts supporting the thought
Facts contradicting the thought
Is this thought based on factual evidence or opinion?

Worksheet available at elemen.com.au

Rather than looking at facts for and against the truth of your thoughts, another very easy approach to reframing your thinking is what is called compassionate cognitive restructuring. Here, you are asked to look at your thoughts in a more compassionate way. Ask yourself what you would say to a person who was in a similar situation to you. In all likelihood, you would say something much kinder and closer to the truth than you are saying to yourself.

Consider this example.

Example	
Your friend says	*One of the other departments in the organisation where I work is being restructured. Even though there has been no talk about my department being restructured, I am worried that I am going to end up being made redundant... although the other department isn't offering redundancies.*
You might say	*It sounds like you don't have anything to worry about. I know the thought of losing your job is scary but it seems that all of these things that are happening are not even happening in the area where you work.*

It is the case that we often are harder on ourselves than others think is necessary. We set higher standards. For example, you might say that you should never make a mistake and call yourself stupid if you do. Your friend would say that everyone makes mistakes, and all we can do is learn from them.

It is interesting that, although you trust your good friends, you choose not to believe them when they make a truthful statement summing up the facts of the situation about which you are worried. Remember how it feels when the reverse occurs when you make a positive statement to your friend, and they dismiss what you say or reject it in favour of a statement you see as false. It is frustrating. You can be as kind and supportive to yourself as you are to the people you care about.

Making the restructured thinking habitual

To get to a point where you are thinking in a healthier way, you need to go through a process of deliberately challenging your thinking. You need to overlearn noticing your automatic thoughts and then reframing them into healthier and more accurate alternative thoughts. You will then challenge your thinking and adjust your automatic thoughts without giving them much attention. Eventually, you will not even have to do that because your core beliefs will be corrected to offer you a more accurate template of how the world works and how you fit into that world.

Targeting the assumptions

Let's not forget about those assumptions that underlie the errors you make in your thinking. You need to challenge those assumptions to completely correct your thinking. Remember, if the assumptions that underlie the error are shown to be wrong, there is every reason to abandon the logical error and replace it with a more logical point of view.

There are a few ways you can challenge the assumptions that underlie logical errors. We are going to focus on three approaches. Firstly, we are going to apply the strategy of looking at the advantages and disadvantages of holding an assumption. Consider the following example of someone who is predicting that things are going to work out poorly.

Logical error and assumption
Catastrophising. Always think the worst because it is most likely to happen to you.
Advantages
I will always be on 'red alert' in case something happens.
Disadvantages
I will be on 'red alert' all the time, even when it is not necessary for me to be so.   *I will find it hard to feel any joy about anything if I constantly worry about everything going wrong.*   *I will waste a lot of time worrying about things that end up not being as bad as I thought they were going to be.*

Challenging the assumption that underlies a tendency to catastrophise, you can see that there are many more disadvantages to doing this than there are advantages. In fact, experiencing the disadvantages may turn out to be worse than the possible thing in the future you are worrying about.

Secondly, you can act against the assumptions. What would happen if the assumption was incorrect? Consider the following example.

Logical error and assumption
Catastrophising. Always think the worst because it is most likely to happen to you.
Things that might happen if I acted like the assumption was not true
I might be able to relax and feel calmer.   *I might find some enjoyment in the things I do.*   *I might experience some peace of mind.*   *I might look forward to some things in the future.*

By acting as if the assumption is false, you can usually identify the positive things that would occur as a consequence. All of these things are better than predicting a gloomy future. Remember, spending your time thinking about how badly things are likely to turn out in the future also removes all the pleasure from the present.

Finally, you can argue against the assumption. You can take the perspective that the assumption is wrong and develop an argument for your case. Consider the following example.

Logical error and assumption
Catastrophising. Always think the worst because it is most likely to happen to you.

Arguments against the assumption
Thinking something might happen will not make it happen.
There is no cosmic force that is directing all bad things my way.

Here, you are thinking of the *facts* that can be used to present a good argument that the assumption associated with the logical error is not accurate. This will allow you to challenge your error-ridden thinking and replace it with healthier thinking that will not encourage you to feel strong, negative emotions. Can you think of other arguments you could use against the assumption?

Below is a worksheet you can use to challenge the assumptions that underlie your errors in thinking.

Targeting assumptions worksheet
Logical error and assumption
Advantages
Disadvantages
Things that might happen if I acted like the assumption was not true
Arguments against the assumption

Worksheet available at elemen.com.au

Here, we have asked you to consider challenging the sorts of thoughts you might have that are likely to make you feel worse than you would otherwise feel if you did not think that way. You have learned to access these logical errors by paying attention to your automatic thoughts that serve as the running commentary your mind provides. You have learned ways to challenge these errors and remove them and their influence from your thinking. The goal of doing these things has been to help you manage your distress and protect yourself from distress in the future.

Some final points

Here are some things that you need to remember.

> Worry occurs because you feel you cannot take a risk and you cannot tolerate uncertainty.
>
> Your worry does nothing to affect the risk of something happening and does not create certainty for you.
>
> Although it feels like you are doing something useful when you worry, all you are doing is making your present existence unpleasant.
>
> Worrying does not solve your problems. There are problem-solving strategies you can use to try to solve your problems, but worry is not one of them.
>
> You can learn to control your worry. You can do this by challenging your thinking, understanding the link between your thinking and how you choose to act, deciding to do things other than worry, controlling your anxiety, and learning to tolerate uncertainty and tolerate acceptable levels of risk.

We wish you well for the future.

Additional reading

Abare, C. (2024). *Unlocking the mind: Understanding anxiety.* Lulu Press.

Clark, D.A., & Beck, A.T. (2012). *The anxiety and worry workbook: The cognitive behavioral solution.* New York: The Guildford Press.

Kennerley, H., Kirk, J., & Westbrook, D. (2016). *An introduction to cognitive behaviour therapy: Skills and applications (3rd edn).* London: Sage Publications.

www.ingramcontent.com/pod-product-compliance
Lightning Source LLC
Chambersburg PA
CBHW080857090426
42735CB00014B/3171